COME AND WELCOME
TO JESUS CHRIST

COME AND WELCOME
TO JESUS CHRIST

John Bunyan

'All that the Father giveth me shall come to me;
and him that cometh to me I will in no wise
cast out' (*John* 6:37).

THE BANNER OF TRUTH TRUST

THE BANNER OF TRUTH TRUST
3 Murrayfield Road, Edinburgh EH12 6EL, UK
P.O. Box 621, Carlisle, PA 17013, USA

*

First Published 1681
First Banner of Truth edition 2004
ISBN 0 85151 853 2

*

Typeset in 10¹/₂/14 pt Sabon at the
Banner of Truth Trust, Edinburgh
Printed and bound in Great Britain
by Bell & Bain Ltd., Glasgow.

Contents

Publisher's Foreword

The Baptist preacher and theologian, Andrew Fuller (1754–1815), was raised under a ministry which had become unbalanced due to its Hyper-Calvinistic emphases. In later years he described his condition, in 1775, as a young pastor:

> The principal writings with which I was first acquainted were those of Bunyan, Gill and Brine. I had read pretty much of Dr Gill's *Body of Divinity*, and from many parts of it had received considerable instruction. I perceived, however, that the system of Bunyan was not the same with his; for that, while he [Bunyan] maintained the doctrines of election and predestination, he nevertheless held with the free offer of salvation to sinners without distinction. These were things which I then could not reconcile, and therefore supposed that Bunyan, though a great and good man, was not so clear in his views of the doctrines of the gospel as the writers who succeeded him. I found, indeed, the same thing in all the old writers of the sixteenth and seventeenth centuries that

came my way. They all dealt, as Bunyan did, in free invitations to sinners to come to Christ and be saved; the consistency of which with personal election I could not understand.

Fuller's subsequent study of this issue resulted in his publication of *The Gospel Worthy of All Acceptation* in 1784, which to a great extent was instrumental in delivering his denomination from the grip of Hyper-Calvinism.[1]

Of all Bunyan's writings, none is so expressive of his delight and joy in the freeness, willingness and graciousness found in Jesus Christ to save sinners as *Come and Welcome to Jesus Christ*. He lists, one after another, all the objections raised by convicted souls who cannot bring themselves to believe that there might be a pardon and a welcome for them in the gospel.

In the variety and diversity of these unbelieving objections we see glimpses of those long years of soul-searching which Bunyan himself experienced. He then demolishes them by his continuous and insistent emphasis that Christ must be taken at his word: that when he cries 'Come!' he means it, whoever it is who hears his call. And in the exuberance of Bunyan's arguments we see surely an indication of the extent to which this truth eventually became his own greatest comfort.

[1] Fuller became the first Secretary of the Baptist Missionary Society, founded in 1792, from which the modern missionary movement grew. He was second only to William Carey in his influence on the Society and its work.

Come and Welcome to Jesus Christ was published in 1681 and was immediately popular – four editions were brought out in the last seven years of Bunyan's life. To read it through is to be convinced again of how well Bunyan understood the human heart, and how well he knew how to encourage many a *Mr Fearing* or *Much-afraid*. We appreciate also why John Owen could make the remark that he would willingly exchange all his learning 'for the tinker's power of touching men's hearts'.

This present edition is taken from the first volume of Bunyan's *Works* (George Offor edition, 1854) which was re-published by the Trust in 1991.[1] The text has been modernized to a limited extent and divided into chapters, but all the divisions correspond to Bunyan's own layout of his material (see the *Analysis* at the end of the book).

THE PUBLISHER
October 2003

---

[1] *The Works of John Bunyan*, three volumes (ISBN 0 85151 598 3), cloth-bound, approximately 800 pp., per volume.

1

The Context and the Text

'All that the Father giveth me shall come to me; and him that cometh to me I will in no wise cast out' (John 6:37).

THE CONTEXT

A little before, in this chapter, you may read that the Lord Jesus walked on the sea to go to Capernaum, having sent his disciples before in a ship, but the wind was contrary; by which means the ship was hindered in her passage. Now, about the fourth watch of the night, Jesus came walking upon the sea, and overtook them; at the sight of whom they were afraid.

Note, when providences are black and terrible to God's people, the Lord Jesus shows himself to them in a wonderful manner; which sometimes they can as little bear as they can the things that were before terrible to them. They were afraid of the wind and the water; they were also afraid of their Lord and Saviour, when he appeared to them in that state.

But he said, 'It is I; be not afraid.'

Note that the purpose of the appearing of the Lord Jesus to his people, though the manner of his appearing might be very terrible, is to allay their fears and perplexities.

'Then they willingly received him into the ship, and immediately the ship was at the land whither they went.'

Note, when Christ is absent from his people, they go on but slowly, and with great difficulty; but when he joins himself to them, oh, how fast they steer their course! How soon are they at their journey's end!

The people now among whom he last preached, when they saw that both Jesus was gone and his disciples, they also took shipping, and came to Capernaum, seeking for Jesus. And when they had found him, they wonderingly asked him, 'Rabbi, when camest thou hither?' but the Lord Jesus, slighting their compliment, answered, 'Verily, verily, ye seek me, not because ye saw the miracles, but because ye did eat of the loaves, and were filled.'

Note, a people may follow Christ far for base motives, as these went after him beyond the sea for loaves. A man's belly will carry him a great way in religion; yes, a man's belly will make him venture far for Christ.

Note again, it is not feigning compliments, but gracious intentions, that crown the work in the eye of Christ; or thus, it is not the toil and business of professors, but their love to him, which makes him approve of them.

Note again, when men shall look for friendly entertainment at Christ's hand, if their hearts are rotten, even then will they meet with a check and rebuke. 'Ye seek me, not because ye saw the miracles, but because ye did eat of the loaves, and were filled.'

Yet observe again, he does not refuse to give, even to these, good counsel: he tells them to labour for the meat that endures to eternal life. Oh! how willingly would Jesus Christ have even those professors that come to him with pretences only, come to him sincerely, that they may be saved.

THE TEXT

The text, you will find, after much more discourse with and about this people, is uttered by the Lord Jesus as the conclusion of the whole. It intimates that, as they were professors in pretence only and therefore such as his soul could not delight in, that he would content himself with a remnant that his Father had bestowed upon him. As if he said, I am not likely to be honoured in your salvation; but the Father has bestowed upon me a people, and they shall come to me in truth, and in them I will be satisfied.

The text, therefore, may be called *Christ's repose*; in the fulfilling of which he rests himself content, after much labour and many sermons spent, as it were, in vain. As he says by the prophet, 'I have laboured in vain, I have spent my strength for nought, and in vain' (*Isa.* 49:4).

But as he says there, 'My judgment is with the LORD, and my work with my God', so in the text he says, 'All that the Father giveth me shall come to me; and him that cometh to me I will in no wise cast out.' By these words, therefore, the Lord Jesus comforts himself under the consideration of the dissimulation of some of his followers. He also thus consoled himself under the consideration of the little effect that his ministry had in Capernaum, Chorazin, and Bethsaida. 'I thank thee, O Father,' said he, 'Lord of heaven and earth, because thou hast hid these things from the wise and prudent, and hast revealed them unto babes; even so, Father, for so it seemed good in thy sight' (*Matt.* 11:25; *Luke* 10:21).

The text, in general, consists of two parts, and has special respect to the Father and the Son; as also to their joint management of the salvation of their people. 'All that the Father giveth me shall come to me; and him that cometh to me I will in no wise cast out.' The first part of the text, as is evident, refers to the Father and his gift; the other part to the Son and his reception of that gift.

Firstly, for *the gift of the Father* there is this to be considered, namely, the gift itself; and that is the gift of certain persons to the Son. The Father gives, and that gift shall come: 'And him that cometh.' The gift, then, is of persons; the Father gives persons to Jesus Christ.

Secondly, next you have *the Son's reception of this gift,* and that shows itself in these particulars:

1. In his hearty acknowledgement of it to be a gift: 'The Father giveth me.'

2. In his taking notice, after a solemn manner, of all and every part of the gift: 'All that the Father giveth me.'

3. In his resolution to bring them to himself: 'All that the Father giveth me shall come to me.'

4. And in his determining that not anything shall make him dislike them in their coming: 'And him that cometh to me I will in no wise cast out.'

These things might be spoken to at large, as they are in this method presented to view: but I shall choose to speak to the words, first, *by way of explanation*; second, *by way of observation*.

2

The Gift and
the Giver

'All that the Father giveth me' (John 6:37).

THE EXTENT OF THE GIFT: 'ALL'

This word *all* is often used in Scripture, and is to be taken more largely or more strictly, according to what the truth or argument, for the sake of which it is made use of, will bear. Therefore, in order that we may the better understand the mind of Christ in the use of it here, we must consider that it is limited and restrained only to those that shall be saved, namely, to those that shall come to Christ; even to those whom he will 'in no wise cast out'. Thus, also, the expression 'all Israel' is sometimes to be taken, although at times it is taken for the whole family of Jacob. 'And so all Israel shall be saved' (*Rom.* 11:26). By all Israel here, he intends not all of Israel, in the largest sense; 'for they are not all Israel, which are of Israel: neither, because they are the seed of Abraham, are they all children: but, In Isaac shall thy seed be called. That is, they which are the children of the flesh, these are not the children of God: but the children of the promise are counted for the seed' (*Rom.* 9:6–8).

This word ALL, therefore, must be limited and enlarged as the truth and argument for the sake of which it is used will bear; otherwise we shall abuse Scripture, and readers, and ourselves, and all. 'And I, if I be lifted up from the earth,' said Christ, 'will draw ALL men unto me' (*John* 12:32). Can any man imagine that by ALL, in this place, he should mean all and every individual man in the world, and not rather all that is consonant to the scope of the place? And if, by being 'lifted up from the earth', he means, as it seems, his being taken up into heaven; and if, by 'drawing ALL men unto him', he meant a drawing them to that place of glory; then must he mean by ALL men, those, and only those, that shall in truth be eternally saved from the wrath to come.

'For God hath concluded them all in unbelief, that he might have mercy upon all' (*Rom.* 11:32). Here again you have *all* and *all*, two *alls*; but yet a greater disparity between the *all* made mention of in the first place, and that *all* made mention of in the second. Those intended in this text are the Jews, even all of them, by the first *all* that you find in the words. The second *all* also intends the same people; but yet only so many of them as God will have mercy upon. 'He has concluded them all in unbelief, that he might have mercy upon all.' The *all* also in the text is likewise to be limited and restrained to the saved, and to them only.

Again, the word 'giveth', or 'has given', must be restrained, after the same manner, to the same limited number. 'All that the Father giveth me.' Not all that are given, if you take the gift of the Father to the Son in the largest sense; for in that sense there are many given to him that shall never come to him; yes, many are given to him that he will 'cast out'. I shall, therefore, first show you the truth of this; and then in what sense the gift in the text must be taken.

First, ALL *cannot be intended in its largest sense.* That ALL that are given to Christ, if you take the gift of the Father to him in the largest sense, cannot be intended in the text, is evident:

1. Because, then, all the men, yes, all the things in the world, must be saved. 'All things', he says, 'are delivered unto me of my Father' (*Matt.* 11:27). This, I think, no rational man in the world will conclude. Therefore, the gift intended in the text must be restrained to some, to a gift that is given by way of speciality by the Father to the Son.

2. It must not be taken for ALL that in any sense are given by the Father to him, because the Father has given some, yes, many to him, to be dashed in pieces by him. 'Ask of me,' said the Father to him, 'and I shall give thee the heathen for thine inheritance, and the uttermost parts of the earth for thy possession.' But what must be done

with them? Must he save them all? No. 'Thou shalt break them with a rod of iron; thou shalt dash them in pieces like a potter's vessel' (*Psa.* 2:8,9). This method he uses not with them that he saves by his grace, but with those that he together with his saints shall rule over in justice and severity (*Rev.* 2:26,27). Yet, as you see, 'they are given to him'. Therefore, the gift intended in the text must be restrained to some, to a gift that is given by way of speciality by the Father to the Son.

In Psalm 18 he says plainly, that some are given to him that he might destroy them. 'Thou hast given me the necks of mine enemies; that I might destroy them that hate me' (verse 40). These, therefore, cannot be of the number of those that are said to be given in the text; for those, even ALL of them, shall come to him, 'and he will in no wise cast them out'.

3. Some are given to Christ that he by them might bring about some of his high and deep designs in the world. Thus Judas was given to Christ, in order that by him, even as was determined before, he might bring about his death, and so the salvation of his elect by his blood. Yes, and Judas must so manage this business, as that he must lose himself for ever in bringing it to pass. Therefore the Lord Jesus, even in his losing of Judas, applies himself to the judgment of his Father, if he had not in that thing done that which was right, even in suffering Judas so to bring about his Master's death that he might, by so doing, bring about his own eternal damnation also.

'Those', said he, 'that thou gavest me, I have kept, and none of them is lost, but the son of perdition; that the Scripture might be fulfilled' (*John* 17:12). Let us, then, grant that Judas was given to Christ, but not as others are given to him, not as those made mention of in the text; for then he should have failed to have been so received by Christ, and kept to eternal life. Indeed, he was given to Christ; but he was given to him to lose him, in the way that I have mentioned before. He was given to Christ, that he by him might bring about his own death, as was before determined; and that in the overthrow of him that did it. Yes, he must bring about his dying for us in the loss of the instrument that betrayed him, that he might even fulfil the Scripture in his destruction, as well as in the salvation of the rest. 'And none of them is lost, but the son of perdition; that the Scripture might be fulfilled.'

Second, *those intended as the gift*. The gift, therefore, in the text, must not be taken in the largest sense, but only according to what the words will bear, namely, for such a gift as he accepts, and promises to be an effectual means of eternal salvation to. 'All that the Father giveth me shall come to me; and him that cometh to me I will in no wise cast out.' Mark! They shall come that are specially given to me; and they shall by no means be rejected. For this is the substance of the text.

Those therefore intended as the gift in the text are those that are given by covenant to the Son. Those that in other places are called 'the elect', 'the chosen', 'the sheep', and 'the children of the promise', etc. These are they that the

Father has given to Christ to keep them; those to whom Christ has promised eternal life; those to whom he has given his word, and that he will have with him in his kingdom to behold his glory.

'This is the Father's will which has sent me, that of all which he hath given me I should lose nothing, but should raise it up again at the last day' (*John* 6:39). 'And I give unto them eternal life; and they shall never perish, neither shall any man pluck them out of my hand. My Father, which gave them me, is greater than all; and no man is able to pluck them out of my Father's hand' (*John* 10:28). 'As thou hast given him power over all flesh, that he should give eternal life to as many as thou hast given him . . . Thine they were, and thou gavest them me, and they have kept thy word; I pray for them: I pray not for the world, but for them which thou hast given me; for they are thine. And all mine are thine, and thine are mine; and I am glorified in them.' 'Keep through thine own name those whom thou hast given me, that they may be one, as we are.' 'Father, I will that they also, whom thou hast given me, be with me where I am; that they may behold my glory, which thou hast given me: for thou lovedst me before the foundation of the world' (*John* 17:1, 6, 9, 10, 24).

All these sentences are of the same meaning as the text; and the *alls* and *manys, those, they,* etc., in these several sayings of Christ, are the same with *all* the given in the text. 'All that the Father giveth.'

So that, as I said before, the word ALL, as also other words, must not be taken in such sort as our foolish fancies or groundless opinions will prompt us to, but admits of an enlargement or a restriction, according to the true meaning and purpose of the text. We must therefore diligently consult the meaning of the text, by comparing it with other sayings of God; so shall we be better able to find out the mind of the Lord, by the Word which he has given us to know it by.

THE PERSON GIVING: THE FATHER

'*All that the Father giveth.*' By this word 'Father', Christ describes the Person giving; by which we may learn several useful things.

1. *That the Lord God, the Father of our Lord Jesus Christ, is concerned with the Son in the salvation of his people.* True, his acts, as to our salvation, are different from those of the Son. He was not capable of doing that, or those things for us, as did the Son. He died not, he spilt not blood for our redemption, as the Son; but yet he has a hand, a great hand, in our salvation too. As Christ says, 'The Father himself loveth you,' and his love is manifest in choosing of us, in giving of us to his Son; yes, and in giving his Son also to be a ransom for us. Hence he is called, 'The Father of mercies, and the God of all comfort.' For here even the Father has himself found out, and made a way for his grace to come to us through the sides and the heart-blood of his well-beloved Son (*Col.* 1:12–14). The Father, therefore, is to be remembered and adored, as one having a chief hand in the salvation of

sinners. We ought to give 'thanks unto the Father, which hath made us meet to be partakers of the inheritance of the saints in light' (*Col.* 1:12). For 'the Father sent the Son to be the Saviour of the world' (*1 John* 4:14). As also we see in the text, 'the Father giveth' the sinner to Christ to save him.

2. *That Christ Jesus the Lord, by this word 'Father', would familiarize this Giver to us.* Naturally the name of God is dreadful to us, especially when he is discovered to us by those names that declare his justice, holiness, power, and glory. But now this word 'Father' is a familiar word, it frightens not the sinner, but rather inclines his heart to love and be pleased with the remembrance of him. Hence Christ also, when he would have us to pray with godly boldness, puts this word 'Father' into our mouths; saying, 'When you pray, say, Our Father which art in heaven', that by the familiarity intimated by such a word, the children of God may take more boldness to pray for, and ask great things.

I myself have often found, that when I can say but this word Father, it does me more good than when I call him by any other Scripture name. It is worth noting, that to call God by his relative title was rare among the saints in Old Testament times. Seldom do you find him called by this name; no, sometimes not in three or four books. But now in New Testament times, he is called by no name so often as this, both by the Lord Jesus himself, and by the apostles afterwards. Indeed, the Lord Jesus was he that first made this name common among the saints, and that taught them, in their discourses, their prayers, and in their writings, to use it much; it being more pleasing to God, and discovering more plainly our interest in him, than any other expression. For by this one name we are made to understand that all our mercies are the offspring of God, and that we also that are called are his children by adoption.

THE MEANING OF THE WORD 'GIVETH'

This word 'giveth' is in Christ's ordinary dialect, and seems to intimate, at the first sound, as if the Father's gift to the Son was not an act that is past, but one that is present and continuing. In truth, this gift was bestowed upon Christ when the covenant, the eternal covenant, was made between them before all worlds. Therefore, in those other places, when this gift is mentioned, it is still spoken of as of an act that is past, as, 'As many as thou hast given me'; 'thou gavest them me'; and 'those which thou hast given me'. Therefore, of necessity, this must be the first and chief sense of the text. The sense, I mean, of this word 'giveth,' otherwise the doctrine of election and of the eternal covenant, which was made between the Father and the Son, in which covenant this gift of the Father is most certainly comprised, will be shaken, or at least questioned, by erroneous and wicked men.

For they may say that the Father gave not all those to Christ that shall be saved, before the world was made, in that this act of giving is an act of continuation.

[14]

But again, this word 'giveth' is not to be rejected, for it has its proper use, and may signify to us,

1. That though the act of giving among men admits of the time past, or the time to come, and is to be spoken of with reference to such time, yet with God it is not so. Things past, or things to come, are always present with God, and with his Son, Jesus Christ. He 'calleth those things which be not,' that is, to us, 'as though they were' (*Rom.* 4:17). And again, 'Known unto God are all his works from the beginning of the world.' All things to God are present, and so is the gift of the Father to the Son, although to us, as is manifest by the word, it is an act that is past (*Acts* 15:18).

2. Christ may express himself thus, to show that the Father has not only given him this portion in the lump, before the world was, but that those that he had so given, he will give him again. That is, he will bring them to him at the time of their conversion; for the Father brings them to Christ (*John* 6:44). As it is said, 'She shall be brought unto the king in raiment of needle-work', that is, in the righteousness of Christ; for it is God that imputes that to those that are saved (*Psa.* 45:14; *1 Cor.* 1:30).

A man gives his daughter to another man, first, *in order to* marriage, and this respects the time past, and he gives her again at the day appointed, *in* marriage. And in this last sense, perhaps, the text may mean that all that the Father has, before the world was, given to Jesus Christ, he gives them again to him in the day of their espousals.

Things that are given among men are often best at first; that is, when they are new; and the reason is, because all earthly things wax old; but with Christ it is not so. This gift of the Father is not old and deformed, and unpleasant in his eyes; and therefore to him it is always new. When the Lord spoke of giving the land of Canaan to the Israelites, he did not say that he had given, or would give it to them, but thus: 'The LORD thy God giveth thee . . . this good land' (*Deut.* 9:6). Not but that he had given it to them, while they were in the loins of their fathers, hundreds of years before. Yet he says now he gives it to them; as if they were now also in the very act of taking possession, when as yet they were on the other side of Jordan. What should the meaning be then? Why, I take it to be this: that the land should be to them always as new; as new as if they were taking possession of it but now. And so is the gift of the Father, mentioned in the text, to the Son; it is always new, as if it were always new.

'*All that the Father giveth me.*' In these words you find mention made of two Persons, the Father and the Son; the Father giving, and the Son receiving or accepting this gift. This, then, in the first place, clearly demonstrates, that the Father and the Son, though they, with the Holy Ghost, are one and the same eternal God, yet, as to their personality, they are distinct. The Father is one, the Son is one, the Holy Spirit is one. But because there is in this text mention made but of two of the three, we will speak only of these two. The giver and receiver cannot be the same person in a proper sense, in the same act of giving and receiving. He that gives, gives not to himself but to another. The Father gives not to the Father (that is, to himself) but to the Son. The Son receives not of the Son (that is, of himself) but of the Father. So when the Father gives commandment, he gives it not to himself, but to another; as Christ says, 'He gave me a commandment' (*John* 12:49). So again, 'I am one that bear witness of myself, and the Father that sent me beareth witness of me' (*John* 8:18).

Further, there is here something that is implied though not expressed, namely, that the Father has not given all men to Christ; that is, in the sense that it is intended in this text (though in a larger sense, as was said before, he has given him every one of them), for then all should be saved. He has, therefore, disposed of some another way. He gives some up to idolatry; he gives some up to uncleanness, to vile affections, and to a reprobate mind. Now these he disposes of in his anger, for their destruction, that they may reap the fruit of their doings, and be filled with the reward of their own ways (*Acts* 7:42; *Rom.* 1:24–28). But neither has he thus disposed of all men; he has even of mercy reserved some from these judgments, and those are they that he will pardon, as he says, 'For I will pardon them whom I reserve' (*Jer.* 50:20). Now these he has given to Jesus Christ, by will, as a legacy and portion. Hence the Lord Jesus says, 'This is the Father's will which hath sent me, that of all which he hath given me I should lose nothing, but should raise it up again at the last day' (*John* 6:39).

THE FATHER'S PURPOSE IN GIVING

The Father, therefore, in giving them to Christ to save them, is declaring to us these following things:

1. *That he is able to answer this design of God*, namely, to save them to the uttermost sin, the uttermost temptation, etc. (*Heb.* 7:25). Hence he is said to lay 'help upon one that is mighty', 'mighty to save' (*Psa.* 89:19; *Isa.* 63:1), and hence it is again that God even of old promised to send his people 'a Saviour, a great one' (*Isa.* 19:20). To save is a great work and calls for almightiness in the undertaker; hence he is called the 'Mighty God, the wonderful Counsellor,' etc. Sin is strong, Satan is also strong, death and the grave are strong, and so is the curse of the law; therefore it follows, that this Jesus must be, by God the Father, accounted almighty, in that he has given his elect to him to save them, and deliver them from these, and that despite all their force and power.

And he gave us testimony of this his might, when he was employed in that part of our deliverance that called for a declaration of it. He abolished death; he destroyed him that had the power of death; he was the destruction of the grave; he has finished sin, and made an end of it, as to its damning effects upon the persons that the Father has given him; he has vanquished the curse of the law, nailed it to his cross, triumphed over them upon his cross, and made a show of these things openly (2 *Tim.* 1:10; *Heb.* 2:14–15; *Hos.* 13:14; *Dan.* 9:24; *Gal.* 3:13; *Col.* 2:14–15). Yes, and even now, as a sign of his triumph and conquest, he is alive from the dead, and has the keys of hell and death in his own keeping (*Rev.* 1:18).

2. *The Father's giving them to him to save them declares to us that he is and will be faithful in his office of Mediator*, and that therefore they shall be secured from the fruit and wages of their sins, which is eternal damnation, by his faithful execution of it. And, indeed, it is said, even by the Holy Ghost himself, that he 'was faithful to him that appointed him', that is, to this work of saving those that the Father has given him for that purpose; as 'Moses was faithful in all his house'. Yes, and more faithful too, for Moses was faithful in God's house but as a servant, 'but Christ as a Son over his own house' (*Heb.* 3). And therefore this man is counted worthy of more glory than Moses, even upon this account, because he was more faithful than he, as well as because of the dignity of his Person.

Therefore in him, and in his truth and faithfulness, God rests well pleased, and has put all the government of this people upon his shoulders. Knowing that nothing shall be wanting in him that may in any way perfect this design. And of this he, the Son, has already given a proof. For when the time was come, that his blood was, by divine justice, required for their redemption, washing, and cleansing, he as freely poured it out of his heart, as if it had been water out of a vessel; not sticking to part with his own life, that the life which was laid up for his people in heaven might not fail to be bestowed upon them. And on this account, as well as upon any other, it is that God calls him 'my righteous servant' (*Isa.* 53:11). For his righteousness could never have been complete, if he had not been to the uttermost faithful to the work he undertook. It is also because he is faithful and true that in righteousness he judges and works for his people's deliverance. He will faithfully perform this trust reposed in him. The Father knows this, and has therefore given his elect to him.

3. *The Father's giving of them to him, to save them declares that he is, and will be, gentle and patient towards them, under all their provocations and miscarriages.* It is not to be imagined, the trials and provocations that the Son of God has all along had with these people that have been given to him that saves them. Indeed he is said to be 'a tried stone', for he has been tried, not only by the devil, guilt of sin, death, and the curse of the law, but also by his people's ignorance, unruliness, falls into sin, and declining to errors in life and doctrine.

Were we but capable of seeing how this Lord Jesus has been tried even by his people, ever since there was one of them in the world, we should be amazed at his patience and gentle behaviour to them. It is said, indeed, 'The LORD is very pitiful, slow to anger, and of great mercy.' And, indeed, if he had not been so, he could never have endured their manners as he has done from Adam until now. Therefore is his pity and bowels towards his church preferred above the pity and bowels of a mother towards her child. 'Can a woman forget her sucking child, that she should not have compassion on the son of her womb?

Yea, they may forget, yet will I not forget thee,' saith the LORD (*Isa*. 49:15).

God did once give Moses, as Christ's servant, a handful of his people, to carry them in his bosom, but no further than from Egypt to Canaan. And this Moses, as is said of him by the Holy Ghost, was the meekest man that was then to be found in the earth. Yes, and he loved the people at a very great rate; yet neither would his meekness nor love hold out in this work. He failed and grew passionate, even to the provoking of his God to anger under this work. 'And Moses said unto the LORD, Wherefore hast thou afflicted thy servant?' But what was the affliction? Why, the Lord had said to him, 'Carry this people in thy bosom as a nursing father beareth the suckling child, unto the land which I swore unto their fathers.' And how then? Not I, says Moses, 'I am not able to bear all this people alone, because it is too heavy for me. If thou deal thus with me, kill me, I pray thee, out of hand . . . and let me not see my wretchedness' (*Num*. 11:11–15).

God gave them to Moses that he might carry them in his bosom, that he might show gentleness and patience towards them, under all the provocations with which they would provoke him from that time till he had brought them to their land. But he failed in the work; he could not exercise it, because he had not sufficient patience towards them. But now it is said of the person speaking in the text, 'He shall gather the lambs with his arm, and carry them in his bosom, and shall gently lead those that are with young' (*Isa*. 40:11). Intimating, that this was one of the qualifications that God looked for, and knew was in him, when he gave his elect to him to save them.

4. *The Father giving him to save them declares that he has sufficient wisdom to contend with all those difficulties that would attend him in his bringing of his sons and daughters to glory.* He made him to us to be wisdom; yes, he is called wisdom itself (*1 Cor.* 1:30). And God says, moreover, that 'he shall deal prudently' (*Isa.* 52:13). And, indeed, he that should take upon him to be the Saviour of the people needed to be wise, because their adversaries are subtle above any. Here they are to encounter with the serpent who for his subtlety outwitted our father and mother, when their wisdom was at its highest (*Gen.* 3). But if we talk of wisdom, our Jesus is wise, wiser than Solomon, wiser than all men, wiser than all angels; he is even the wisdom of God. Christ is 'the wisdom of God' (*1 Cor.* 1:24). And hence it is that he turns sin, temptations, persecutions, falls, and all things, for good to his people (*Rom.* 8:28).

Now these things which have been discussed show us also the great and wonderful love of the Father, in that he should choose out this one way so well prepared for the work of man's salvation.

Herein, indeed, perceive we the love of God. Huram gathered that God loved Israel because he had given them such a king as Solomon (*2 Chron.* 2:11). But how much more may we behold the love that God has bestowed upon us, in that he has given us to his Son, and also given his Son for us?

3

Coming to Christ

'*All that the Father giveth me* SHALL COME'
(John 6:37).

In these last words there is closely inserted an answer to
the Father's purpose in giving his elect to Jesus Christ.
The Father's purpose was that they might come to him,
and be saved by him; and that, says the Son, shall be
done; neither sin nor Satan, neither flesh nor world,
neither wisdom nor folly, shall hinder their coming to me.
'They shall come to me; and him that cometh to me I will
in no wise cast out.'

Here, therefore, the Lord Jesus positively determines to
put forth such a sufficiency of all grace as shall effectually
perform this promise. 'They shall come'; that is, he will
cause them to come, by infusing an effectual blessing into
all the means that shall be used to that end. It was said to
the evil spirit that was sent to persuade Ahab to go and

fall at Ramoth-Gilead, 'Thou shalt persuade him, and prevail also: go forth, and do so' (*1 Kings* 22:22). So will Jesus Christ say of the means that shall be used for the bringing of those to him that the Father has given him. I say, he will bless it effectually to this very end; it shall persuade them, and shall prevail also. Otherwise, as I said, the Father's purpose would be frustrated; for the Father's will is that 'of all which he has given him, he should lose nothing, but should raise it up at the last day' (*John* 6:39), in order next to himself, Christ the first-fruits, afterwards those that are his at his coming (*1 Cor.* 15). But this cannot be done if there should fail to be a work of grace effectually wrought, though but in any one of them. But this shall not fail to be wrought in them, even in all the Father has given him to save. 'All that the Father has given me shall come unto me'.

But to speak more distinctly to the words: THEY 'SHALL COME': two things I would show you from these words, First, *what it is to come to Christ*. Second, *what force there is in this promise, to make them come to him*.

WHAT IT IS TO COME TO CHRIST

Firstly, I would show you *what it is to come to Christ*. This word *come* must be understood spiritually, not carnally; for many came to him carnally, or bodily, that had no saving advantage by him. Multitudes came to him thus in the days of his flesh; yes, innumerable companies. There is also at this day a formal coming out of habit to his ordinances and ways of worship, which avails not anything; but with them I shall not now meddle, for they are not intended in the text. The coming, then, intended in the text is to be understood of the coming of the mind to him, even the moving of the heart towards him. I say the moving of the heart towards him, from a sound sense of the absolute want that a man has of him for his justification and salvation.

This description of coming to Christ divides itself into two heads: First, that coming to Christ is *a moving of the mind towards him*. Second, that it is a moving of the mind towards him, *from a sound sense of the absolute want that a man has of him for his justification and salvation*.

First, that it is *a moving of the mind towards him*: this is evident, because coming here or there, if it is voluntary, is by an act of the mind or will; so coming to Christ is through the inclining of the will. 'Thy people shall be willing' (*Psa.* 110:3). This willingness of heart is what sets the mind moving after or towards him. The church expresses this moving of her mind towards Christ by the moving of her bowels. 'My beloved put in his hand by the hole of the door, and my bowels were moved for him' (*Song of Sol.* 5:4). 'My bowels' indicates the passions of my mind and affections; which passions of the affections are expressed by the yearning and sounding of the bowels, the yearning or passionate working of them, the sounding of them, or their making a noise for him (*Gen.* 43:30; *1 Kings* 3:26; *Isa.* 16:11).

This, then, is the coming to Christ, even a moving towards him with the mind. 'And it shall come to pass, that every thing that liveth, which moveth, whithersoever the rivers shall come, shall live' (*Ezek.* 47:9). The water in this text is the grace of God in the doctrine of it. The living things are the children of men, to whom the grace of God, by the gospel, is preached. Now, he says, every living thing which moves, whithersoever the water shall come, shall live.

And notice how this word *moveth* is expounded by Christ himself, in the book of Revelation: 'The Spirit and the bride say, Come. And let him that heareth say, Come. And let him that is athirst come. And whosoever will,' that is, *is willing*, 'let him take the water of life freely' (*Rev.* 22:17).

So that to move in your mind and will after Christ is to be coming to him. There are many poor souls that are coming to Christ that yet cannot tell how to believe it, because they think that coming to him is some strange and wonderful thing; and, indeed, so it is. But I mean, they overlook the inclination of their will, the moving of their mind, and the sounding of their bowels after him; and do not count these as part of this strange and wonderful thing. Rather, indeed, it is a work of greatest wonder in this world, to see a man who was once dead in sin, possessed of the devil, an enemy to Christ and to all things spiritually good; I say, to see this man moving with his mind after the Lord Jesus Christ, is one of the highest wonders in the world.

Second, it is a moving of the mind towards him, *from a sound sense of the absolute want that a man has of him for his justification and salvation.* Indeed, without this sense of a lost condition without him, there will be no moving of the mind towards him.

A moving of their mouth there may be; 'With their mouth they show much love' (*Ezek.* 33:31). Such a people as this will come as the true people come; that is, in show and outward appearance. And they will sit before God's ministers, as his people sit before them; and they will hear his words too, but they will not do them; that is, will not come inwardly with their minds. 'For with their mouth they shew much love, but their heart', or mind, 'goeth after their covetousness.' Now, all this is because they lack an effectual sense of the misery of their state by nature; for not till they have that will they, in their mind, move after him.

Therefore, thus it is said concerning the true comers, 'In that day . . . the great trumpet shall be blown, and they shall come which were ready to perish in the land of Assyria, and the outcasts in the land of Egypt, and shall worship the LORD in the holy mount at Jerusalem' (*Isa.* 27:13). They are then, as you see, the outcasts, and those that are ready to perish, that, indeed, have their minds effectually moved to come to Jesus Christ. This sense of things was that which made the three thousand come, that made Saul come, that made the jailor come, and that, indeed, makes all others come, who come effectually (*Acts* chapters 2, 9 and 16).

Of the true coming to Christ, the four lepers were a famous example, of whom you read in 2 Kings 7:3, etc. The famine in those days was sore in the land. There was no bread for the people; and as for that sustenance that was, which was asses' flesh and doves' dung, that was only in Samaria, and of these the lepers had no share, for they were thrust without the city. Well, now they sat in the gate of the city, and hunger was, as I may say, making his last meal of them; and being, therefore, half dead already, what do they think of doing? Why, first they display the dismal colours of death before each other's faces, and then resolve what to do, saying, 'If we say we will enter into the city, then famine is in the city, and we shall die there: if we sit still here, we die also. Now, therefore, come, let us fall unto the host of the Syrians: if they save us alive, we shall live; if they kill us, we shall but die.'

Here, now, was necessity at work, and this necessity drove them to go there for life, otherwise they would never have gone for it. Thus it is with them that in truth come to Jesus Christ. Death is before them, they see it and feel it; he is feeding upon them, and will eat them quite up, if they come not to Jesus Christ; and therefore they come, even of necessity, being forced to it by that sense they have of their being utterly and everlastingly undone, if they do not find safety in him. These are they that will come. Indeed, these are they that are invited to come. 'Come unto me, all ye that labour and are heavy laden, and I will give you rest' (*Matt.* 11:28).

Take two or three things to make this more plain; namely, that coming to Christ flows from a sound sense of the absolute need that a man has of him.

1. 'They shall come with weeping, and with supplications will I lead them; I will cause them to walk by the rivers of waters in a straight way wherein they shall not stumble' (*Jer.* 31:9). Mind it; they come with weeping and supplication; they come with prayers and tears. Now prayers and tears are the effects of a right sense of the need of mercy. Thus a senseless sinner cannot come, he cannot pray, he cannot cry, he cannot come sensible of what he does not see or feel. 'In those days, and in that time . . . the children of Israel shall come; they and the children of Judah together, going and weeping: they shall go and seek the LORD their God. They shall ask the way to Zion with their faces thitherward, saying, Come and let us join ourselves to the LORD in a perpetual covenant that shall not be forgotten' (*Jer.* 50:4–5).

2. This coming to Christ is called a *running* to him, as *flying* to him; a fleeing to him from wrath to come. By all these terms is set forth the condition of the man that comes; namely, that he is affected with the sense of his sin, and the death due to it; that he is sensible that the avenger of blood pursues him, and that, therefore, he is thus lost, if he does not speed to the Son of God for life (*Matt.* 3:7; *Psa.* 143:9). Flying is the last work of a man in danger; all that are in danger do not fly; no, not all that see themselves in danger; flying is the last work of a man in

danger; all that hear of danger will not fly. Men will consider if there be no other way of escape before they fly. Therefore, as I said, flying is the last thing. When all refuge fails, and a man is made to see that there is nothing left him but sin, death, and damnation, unless he flies to Christ for life, then he flies, and not till then.

3. That the true coming is from a sense of an absolute need of Jesus Christ to save, etc., is evident by the outcry that is made by them to come, even as they are coming to him, 'Lord, save me, or I perish'; 'Men and brethren, what shall we do?' 'Sirs, what must I do to be saved?' and the like (*Matt.* 14:30; *Acts* 2:37; 16:30). This language sufficiently discovers that the truly-coming souls are souls sensible of their need of salvation by Jesus Christ; and, moreover, that there is nothing else that can help them but Christ.

4. It is yet further evident by these few things that follow: it is said that such are 'pricked in their heart,' that is, with the sentence of death by the law; and the least prick in the heart kills a man (*Acts* 2:37). Such are said, as I said before, to weep, to tremble, and to be astonished in themselves at the evident and unavoidable danger that attends them, unless they fly to Jesus Christ (*Acts* 9:6).

5. Coming to Christ is attended with an honest and sincere forsaking of all for him. 'If any man come to me, and hate not his father and mother, and wife, and children, and brethren, and sisters, yea, and his own life also, he cannot be my disciple. And whosoever does not bear

his cross, and come after me, cannot be my disciple' (*Luke* 14:26–27).

By these and the like expressions elsewhere, Christ describes the *true comer*, or the man that indeed is coming to him. He is one that casts all behind his back; he leaves all, he forsakes all, he hates all things that would stand in his way to hinder his coming to Jesus Christ. There are a great many pretended comers to Jesus Christ in the world; and they are very much like the man you read of in Matthew 21:30, that said to his father's bidding, 'I go, Sir,' and went not.

I say, there are a great many such comers to Jesus Christ; they say, when Christ calls by his gospel, I come, Sir; but still they abide by their pleasures and carnal delights. They come not at all, only they give him a courtly compliment; but he takes notice of it, and will not let it pass for anything other than a lie. He said, 'I go, Sir,' and went not; he dissembled and lied.

Take heed of this, you that flatter yourselves with your own deceivings. Words will not do with Jesus Christ. Coming is coming, and nothing else will pass for coming with him.

OBJECTIONS THAT USUALLY LIE IN THE WAY OF COMING TO CHRIST

Before I speak to the other head, I shall answer some objections that usually lie in the way of those that in truth are coming to Jesus Christ.

OBJECTION 1: 'Though I cannot deny but my mind runs after Christ, and that, too, out of a sight and consideration of my lost condition, for I see without him I perish; yet I fear my motives are not right in coming to him.'

QUESTION: Why, what is your motive in coming to Christ?

ANSWER: My motive is, that I might have life, and be saved by Jesus Christ.

This is the objection. Well, let me tell you, that to come to Christ for life, and to be saved, although at present you have no other motive, is a lawful and good coming to Jesus Christ. This is evident, because Christ offers life as the only argument to prevail with sinners to come to him, and so also blames them because they do not come to him for life. 'And ye will not come to me, that ye might have life' (*John* 5:40). Besides, there are many other Scriptures by which he allures sinners to come to him, in which he offers nothing to them but their safety. As, 'Whosoever believeth in him should not perish;' he that believeth is 'passed from death unto life'. 'He that believeth . . . shall be saved.' 'He that believeth on him is not condemned.' And believing and coming are all one. So that you see, to come to Christ for life, is a lawful coming and good, in that he believes, that he alone has made atonement for sin (*Rom.* 5). And let me add, over and above, that for a man to come to Christ for life, though he comes to him for nothing else but life, it is to give much honour to him.

1. *He honours the Word of Christ*, and consents to the truth of it; and that in these two general heads.

i. He consents to the truth of all those sayings that testify that sin is most abominable in itself, dishonourable to God, and damnable to the soul of man; for thus says the man that comes to Jesus Christ (*Jer.* 44:4; *Rom.* 2:23; 6:23; *2 Thess.* 2:12).

ii. In that he believes, as the Word has said, that there is in the world's best things, righteousness and all, nothing but death and damnation; for so also says the man that comes to Jesus Christ for life (*Rom.* 7:24–25; 8:2–3; *2 Cor.* 3:6–8).

2. *He honours Christ's Person*, in that he believes that there is life in him, and that he is able to save him from death, hell, the devil, and damnation; for unless a man believes this, he will not come to Christ for life (*Heb.* 7:24–25).

3. *He honours his mission,* in that he believes that he is authorized of the Father to give life to those that come to him for it (*John* 5:11–12; 17:1–3).

4. *He honours the priesthood of Jesus Christ:*

i. In that he believes that Christ has more power to save from sin by the sacrifice that he has offered for it, than has all law, devils, death, or sin to condemn. He that believes not this, will not come to Jesus Christ for life (*Acts* 13:38; *Heb.* 2:14–15; *Rev.* 1:17–18).

ii. In that he believes that Christ, according to his office, will be most faithful and merciful in the discharge of his office. This must be included in the faith of him that comes for life to Jesus Christ (*1 John* 2:1–3; *Heb.* 2:17–18).

5. Further, he that comes to Jesus Christ for life *takes part with him* against sin, and against the ragged and imperfect righteousness of the world; yes, and against false Christs, and damnable errors, that set themselves against the worthiness of his merits and sufficiency. This is evident, for that such a soul singles Christ out from them all, as the only one that can save.

6. Therefore as Noah, at God's command, *you prepare this ark, for the saving of yourself,* by which also you condemn the world, and have become heir of the righteousness which is by faith (*Heb.* 11:7). Therefore, coming sinner, be content; he that comes to Jesus Christ, believes too that he is willing to show mercy to, and have compassion upon him, though unworthy, that comes to him for life. And therefore your soul lies not only under a special invitation to come, but under a promise too of being accepted and forgiven (*Matt.* 11:28).

All these particular parts and qualities of faith are in that soul that comes to Jesus Christ for life, as is evident to any indifferent judgment. For, will he that believes not the testimony of Christ concerning the baseness of sin, and the insufficiency of the righteousness of the world, come to Christ for life? No. He that believes not this testimony of the Word, comes not. He that believes that there is life anywhere else, comes not. He that questions whether the Father has given Christ power to forgive, comes not. He that thinks that there is more in sin, in the law, in death, and the devil, to destroy, than there is in Christ to save, comes not. He also that questions his faithful management of his priesthood for the salvation of sinners, comes not.

You, then, who are indeed the coming sinner, believe all this. True, perhaps you do not believe with that full assurance, nor have you leisure to take notice of your faith as to these distinct acts of it; but yet all this faith is in him who comes to Christ for life. And the faith that thus works is the faith of the best and purest kind; because this man comes alone as a sinner, and as seeing that life is, and is to be had, only in Jesus Christ.

Before I conclude my answer to this objection, take into your consideration these two things.

Firstly, consider that the *cities of refuge* were erected for those that were dead in law, and that yet would live by grace; even for those that were to fly there for life from the avenger of blood that pursued after them. And it is worth your noting that those that were upon their flight there are in a peculiar manner called the people of God: 'Cast ye up, cast ye up,' says God; 'prepare the way; take up the stumblingblock out of the way of my people' (*Isa.* 57:14). This is meant of preparing the way to the city of refuge, that the slayers might escape there; which flying slayers are here, specifically, called the people of God; even those of them that escaped there for life.

Secondly, consider that of *Ahab*, when Benhadad sent to him for life, saying, 'Thus saith your servant Benhadad, I pray you let me live.' Though Benhadad had sought the crown, kingdom, yes, and also the life of Ahab, yet how effectually does Benhadad prevail with him! Is Benhadad yet alive? says Ahab; He is my brother; yea, go ye, bring him to me. So he made him ride in his chariot (*1 Kings* 20).

Coming sinner, what do you think? If Jesus Christ had as little goodness in him as Ahab, he might grant a humble Benhadad life; you neither begged of him his crown and dignity; life, eternal life, will serve your turn. How much more then shall you have it, since you have to deal with him who is goodness and mercy itself! Yes, since you are also called upon, yes, greatly encouraged by a promise of life, to come to him for life! Read also these Scriptures: Numbers 35:11,14,15; Joshua 20:1–6; Hebrews 6:16–21.

OBJECTION 2: 'When I say I only seek myself, I mean I do not find that I design God's glory in my own salvation by Christ, and that makes me fear I do not come aright.'

ANSWER: Where does Christ Jesus require such a qualification of those that are coming to him for life? Come for life, and trouble not your head with such objections against yourself, and let God and Christ alone to glorify themselves in the salvation of such a worm as yourself.

The Father says to the Son, 'Thou art my servant, O Israel, in whom I will be glorified.' God offers life to sinners, as the argument to prevail with them to come to him for life; and Christ says plainly, 'I am come that they might have life' (*John* 10:10). He has no need of your designs, though you have need of his. Eternal life, pardon of sin, and deliverance from wrath to come, Christ offers to you, and these are the things that you have need of. Besides, God will be gracious and merciful to worthless, undeserving wretches. Come then as such a one, and lay no stumblingblocks in the way to him, but come to him for life, and live (*John* 5:34; 10:10; 3:36; *Matt.* 1:21; *Prov.* 8:35–36; *1 Thess.* 1:10; *John* 11:25–26).

When the jailor said, 'Sirs, what must I do to be saved?' Paul did not so much as once ask him, What is your motive in this question? Do you design the glory of God, in the salvation of your soul? He had more sense; he knew that such questions as these would have been but foolish talk, instead of a sufficient relief to so weighty a question as this. Therefore, since this poor wretch lacked salvation by Jesus Christ, the salvation from hell and death, which he knew, now, was due to him for the sins that he had committed, Paul tells him, as the poor condemned sinner that he was, to proceed still in this his way of self-seeking, saying, 'Believe on the Lord Jesus Christ, and thou shalt be saved' (*Acts* 16:30–32).

I know that afterwards you will desire to glorify Christ by walking in the way of his precepts; but at present you want life; the avenger of blood is behind you, and the devil like a roaring lion is behind you; well, come now, and obtain life from these; and when you have obtained some comfortable persuasion that you are made partaker of life by Christ, then, and not till then, you will say, 'Bless the LORD, O my soul, and all that is within me bless his holy name. Bless the LORD, O my soul, and forget not all his benefits: who forgiveth all thine iniquities, who healeth all thy diseases; who redeemeth thy life from destruction; who crowneth thee with lovingkindness and tender mercies' (*Psa.* 103:1–4).

OBJECTION 3: 'But I cannot believe that I come to Christ aright, because sometimes I am apt to question his very being and office to save.'

ANSWER: Thus to do is horrible; but may you not be judging amiss in this matter?

'How can I judge amiss, when I judge as I feel?'

Poor soul! You may judge amiss for all that.

'Why,' says the sinner, 'I think that these questionings come from my heart.'

Let me answer. That which comes from your heart, comes from your will and affections, from your understanding, judgment, and conscience, for these must acquiesce in your questioning, if your questioning be with your heart. And how do you say, for to name no more, do you with your affection and conscience thus question?

'No, my conscience trembles when such thoughts come into my mind; and my affections are otherwise inclined.'

Then I conclude that these things are either suddenly injected by the devil, or else are the fruits of that body of sin and death that yet dwells within you, or perhaps from both together. If they come wholly from the devil, as they seem, because your conscience and affections are against them, or if they come from that body of death that is in you (and do not be curious in inquiring from which of them they come, the safest way is to lay enough at your own door), nothing of this should hinder your coming, nor make you conclude you do not come aright. And before I leave you, let me query with you a little about this matter.

1. Do you like these wicked blasphemies?

Answer: 'No, no, their presence and working kills me.'

2. Do you mourn for them, pray against them, and hate yourself because of them?

Answer: 'Yes, yes; but that which afflicts me is, I do not prevail against them.'

3. Do you sincerely choose, if you could have your choice, that your heart might be affected and taken with the things that are best, most heavenly, and holy?

Answer: 'With all my heart, and death the next hour, if it were God's will, rather than thus to sin against him.'

Well then, your not liking of them, your mourning for them, your praying against them, and your loathing yourself because of them, with your sincere choosing of those thoughts for your delight that are heavenly and holy, clearly declares, that these things are not countenanced either by your will, affections, understanding, judgment, or conscience; and so, that your heart is not in them. They come immediately from the devil, or arise from the body of death that is in your flesh, of which you ought thus to say, 'Now, then, it is no more I that do it, but sin that dwelleth in me' (*Rom.* 7:17).

I will give you a pertinent example. In Deuteronomy 22, you may read of a betrothed damsel, one betrothed to her beloved, one that had given him her heart and mouth, as you have given yourself to Christ. But she was met with as she walked in the field, by one that forced her, because he was stronger than she. Well, what judgment now does God, the righteous judge, pass upon the damsel for this? 'The man only that lay with her', says God, 'shall die. But unto the damsel you shall do nothing; there is in the damsel no sin worthy of death. For, as when a man rises against his neighbour, and slays him, even so is this matter; for he found her in the field, and the betrothed damsel cried, and there was none to save her' (*Deut.* 22:25-27).

You are this damsel. The man that forced you with these blasphemous thoughts, is the devil; and he lights upon you in a fit place, even in the field, as you are wandering after Jesus Christ; but you cried out, and by your cry did show, that you abhorred such wicked lewdness. Well, the Judge of all the earth will do right; he will not lay the sin at your door, but at his that offered the violence. And for your comfort take this into consideration, that he came to heal them 'that were oppressed of the devil' (*Acts* 10:38).

OBJECTION 4: 'But', says another, 'I am so heartless, so slow, and, as I think, so indifferent in my coming, that, to speak truth, I know not whether my kind of coming ought to be called a coming to Christ.'

ANSWER: You know that I told you at first that coming to Christ is a moving of the heart and affections towards him.

'But', says the soul, 'my dullness and indifference in all holy duties, demonstrate my heartlessness in coming; and to come, and not with the heart, signifies nothing at all.'

1. The moving of the heart after Christ is not to be discerned, at all times, by your sensible affectionate performance of duties, but rather by those secret groanings and complaints which your soul makes to God against that sloth that attends you in duties.

2. But grant it to be even as you say it is, that you come so slowly, etc., yet, since Christ bids them come that come not at all, surely they may be accepted that come, though attended with those infirmities which you at present groan under. He says, 'And him that cometh'. He says not, If they come sensibly, and so fast; but, 'And him that cometh to me I will in no wise cast out.' He says also in Proverbs 9, 'As for him that wanteth understanding' (that is, a heart, for often the understanding is taken for the heart), 'come, eat of my bread, and drink of the wine which I have mingled.'

3. You may be vehement in your spirit in coming to Jesus Christ, and yet be plagued with sensible sloth. So was the church when she cried, 'Draw me, we will run after thee', and Paul, when he said, 'When I would do good, evil is present with me' (*Song of Sol.* 1:4; *Rom.* 7; *Gal.* 5:19). The works, strugglings, and oppositions of the flesh are more manifest than the works of the Spirit in our hearts, and so are sooner felt than they. What then? Let us not be discouraged at the sight and feeling

of our own infirmities, but run the faster to Jesus Christ for salvation.

4. Get your heart warmed with the sweet promise of Christ's acceptance of the coming sinner, and that will make you hasten more to him. Discouraging thoughts are like cold weather, they numb the senses, and make us go awkwardly about our business; but the sweet and warm glowings of promise are like the comfortable beams of the sun, which liven and refresh. You see how little the bee and the fly play in the air in winter. Why, the cold hinders them from doing it; but when the wind and sun is warm, who so busy as they?

5. But again, he that comes to Christ flies for his life. Now, there is no man that flies for his life that thinks he speeds fast enough on his journey; no, could he, he would willingly take a mile at a step. 'Oh, my sloth and heartlessness!', you say. 'Oh that I had wings like a dove! for then would I fly away, and be at rest . . . I would hasten my escape from the windy storm and tempest' (*Psa.* 55:6, 8).

Poor coming soul, you are like the man that would ride full gallop, whose horse will hardly trot! Now, the desire of his mind is not to be judged by the slow pace of the dull jade he rides on, but by the hitching, and kicking, and spurring, as he sits on his back. Your flesh is like this dull jade; it will not gallop after Christ; it will be backward, though your soul and heaven lie at stake. But be of good comfort, Christ judges not according to the fierceness of outward motion (*Mark* 10:17) but according to the sincerity of the heart and inward parts (*John* 1:47; *Psa.* 51:6; *Matt.* 26:41).

6. Ziba, in appearance, came to David much faster than did Mephibosheth; but yet his heart was not so upright in him to David as was his. It is true, Mephibosheth had a check from David; for, said he, 'Why wentest not you with me, Mephibosheth?' But when David came to remember that Mephibosheth was lame, for that was his plea: 'Thy servant is lame' (*2 Sam.* 19), he was content, and concluded he would have come after him faster than he did; and Mephibosheth appealed to David, who was in those days as an angel of God, to know all things that are done in the earth, if he did not believe that the reason of his backwardness lay in his lameness and not in his mind.

Why, poor coming sinner, you cannot come to Christ with that outward swiftness of a courier as many others do; but does the reason of your backwardness lie in your mind and will, or in the sluggishness of the flesh? Can you say sincerely, 'The spirit indeed is willing, but the flesh is weak' (*Matt.* 26:41). Yes, can you appeal to the Lord Jesus, who knows perfectly the very inmost thought of your heart, that this is true? Then take this for your comfort, he has said, 'I will assemble her that halteth . . . I will make her that halted a remnant' (*Mic.* 4:6), 'And I will save her that halteth' (*Zeph.* 3:19). What more can you have from the sweet lips of the Son of God?

7. I read of some that are to follow Christ in chains; I

say, to come after him in chains. 'Thus saith the LORD, The labour of Egypt, and merchandise of Ethiopia and of the Sabeans, men of stature, shall come over unto thee, and they shall be thine: they shall come after thee: in chains they shall come over, and they shall fall down unto thee: they shall make supplication unto thee, saying, Surely . . . there is none else [to save]' (*Isa.* 45:14). Surely they that come after Christ in chains come to him in great difficulty, because their steps, by the chains, are straitened. And what chains are so heavy as those that discourage you? Your chain, which is made up of guilt and filth, is heavy; it is a wretched bond about your neck, by which your strength fails (*Lam.* 1:14; 3:18).

But come, though you come in chains, it is glory to Christ that a sinner comes after him in chains. The chinking of your chains, though troublesome to you, is not, nor can be obstruction to your salvation. It is Christ's work and glory to save you from your chains, to enlarge your steps, and set you at liberty. The blind man, though called, surely could not come apace to Jesus Christ, but Christ could stand still, and stay for him (*Mark* 10:49). True, 'He rideth upon the wings of the wind', but yet he is long-suffering, and his long-suffering is salvation to him that cometh to him (2 *Pet.* 3:9).

8. Had you seen those that came to the Lord Jesus in the days of his flesh, how slowly, how hobblingly, they came to him, by reason of their infirmities, and also how friendly and kindly and graciously he received them, and

gave them the desire of their hearts, you would not, as you do, make such objections against yourself, in your coming to Jesus Christ.

OBJECTION 5: 'But', says another, 'I fear I come too late; I doubt I have stayed too long; I am afraid the door is shut.'

ANSWER: You can never come too late to Jesus Christ, if you do come. This is manifest by two instances.

1. By the man that came to him at the eleventh hour. This man was idle all the day long. He had a whole gospel day to come in, and he played it all away except for the last hour only. But at last, at the eleventh hour, he came, and went into the vineyard to work with the rest of the labourers, that had borne the burden and heat of the day. Well, but how was he received by the lord of the vineyard? Why, when pay day came, he had even as much as the rest; yes, had his money first. True, the others murmured at him; but what did the Lord Jesus answer them? 'Is thine eye evil, because I am good? I will give unto this last, even as unto you' (*Matt.* 20:14–15).

2. The other instance is the thief upon the cross. He came late also, only an hour before his death. Yes, he stayed from Jesus Christ as long as he had liberty to be a thief, and longer too; for could he have deluded the judge, and by lying words have escaped his just condemnation, for all I know, he would not yet have come to his Saviour; but being convicted, and condemned to die, yes, fastened

to the cross, that he might die like a rogue, as he was in his life; behold the Lord Jesus, when this wicked one, even now, desired mercy at his hands, tells him, and that without the least reflection upon him, for his former misspent life, 'To day shalt thou be with me in paradise' (*Luke* 23:43). Let no man turn this grace of God into wantonness. My design is now to encourage the coming soul.

OBJECTION: But is not the door of mercy shut against some before they die?

ANSWER: Yes; and God forbids that prayers should be made to him for them (*Jer.* 6:16; *Jude* 22).

QUESTION: Then, may I not be one of these?

ANSWER: By no means, if you are coming to Jesus Christ; because when God shuts the door upon men, he gives them no heart to come to Jesus Christ. None come but those to whom it is given of the Father. But you are coming, therefore it is given to you of the Father.

Be sure, therefore, that if the Father has given you a heart to come to Jesus Christ, the gate of mercy still stands open to you. For it stands not with the wisdom of God to give strength to come to the birth, and yet to shut up the womb (*Isa.* 66:9); to give grace to come to Jesus Christ, and yet shut up the door of his mercy upon you. 'Incline your ear,' says he, 'and come unto me: hear, and your soul shall live; and I will make an everlasting covenant with you, even the sure mercies of David' (*Isa.* 55:3).

OBJECTION: But it is said that some knocked when the door was shut.

ANSWER: Yes, but the texts in which these knockers are mentioned, are to be referred to the day of judgment, and not to the coming of the sinner to Christ in this life. See the texts, *Matt.* 15:11; *Luke* 13:24–25. These, therefore, do not concern you at all, you who are coming to Jesus Christ; you are coming NOW! 'Now is the accepted time; behold, now is the day of salvation' (*2 Cor.* 6:2). Now God is upon the mercy-seat; now Christ Jesus sits by, continually pleading the victory of his blood for sinners; and now, even as long as this world lasts, this word of the text shall still be free, and fully fulfilled; 'And him that cometh to me I will in no wise cast out.'

Sinner, the greater sinner you are, the greater need of mercy you have, and the more will Christ be glorified thereby. Come then, come and try; come, taste and see how good the Lord is to an undeserving sinner!

OBJECTION 6: 'But', says another, 'I am fallen since I began to come to Christ; therefore I fear I did not come aright, and so consequently that Christ will not receive me.'

ANSWER: Falls are dangerous, for they dishonour Christ, wound the conscience, and cause the enemies of God to speak reproachfully. But it is no good argument, I am fallen, therefore I was not coming aright to Jesus Christ. If David, Solomon and Peter had thus objected against themselves, they had added to their griefs; and yet, at least they had as much cause as you. A man whose steps are ordered by the Lord, and whose goings the Lord delights in, may yet be overtaken with a temptation that may cause him to fall (*Psa.* 37:23–24). Did not Aaron fall, yes, and Moses himself? What shall we say of Hezekiah and Jehoshaphat? There are, therefore, falls and falls; falls pardonable and falls unpardonable. Falls unpardonable are falls against light, from the faith, to the despising of and trampling upon Jesus Christ and his blessed undertakings (*Heb.* 6:2–6; 10:28–29). Now, as for such, there remains no more sacrifice for sin. Indeed, they have no heart, no mind, no desire to come to Jesus Christ for life, therefore they must perish. Nay, says the Holy Ghost, 'It is impossible that they should be renewed again unto repentance.'

Therefore these God had no compassion for, neither ought we; but for other falls though they be dreadful, and God will chastise his people for them, they do not prove you a graceless man, one not coming to Jesus Christ for life.

It is said of the child in the gospel, that while 'he was yet a coming, the devil threw him down, and tare him' (*Luke* 9:42). Dejected sinner, it is no wonder that you have caught a fall in coming to Jesus Christ. Is it not rather to be wondered at, that you have not caught before this a thousand times a thousand falls? When we consider: 1. What fools we are by nature. 2. What weaknesses are in us. 3. What mighty powers the fallen angels, our implacable enemies, are. 4. Considering also how often the coming man is benighted in his journey; and also what stumblingblocks do lie in his way. 5. Also his friends, that were so before, now watch for his halting, and seek by what means they may cause him to fall by the hand of their strong ones.

What then? Must we, because of these temptations, incline to fall? No. Must we not fear falls? Yes. 'Let him that thinketh he standeth take heed lest he fall' (*1 Cor.* 10:12). Yet let him not utterly be cast down; 'The LORD upholdeth all that fall, and raiseth up those that are bowed down.' Make not light of falls! Yet, have you fallen? 'Ye have', said Samuel, 'done all this wickedness; yet turn not aside from following the LORD', but serve him with a perfect heart, and turn not aside, 'for the LORD will not forsake his people', and he counts the coming sinner one of them, 'because it hath pleased the LORD to make you his people' (*1 Sam.* 12:20–22).

WHAT FORCE THERE IS IN THIS PROMISE TO MAKE THEM COME TO HIM

Now we come to show what force there is in this promise to make them come to him: 'All that the Father giveth me shall come to me.' I will speak to this promise, firstly, in general, secondly, in particular.

Firstly, *in general*. This word SHALL is confined to these ALL that are given to Christ. 'All that the Father giveth me shall come to me.' Hence I conclude,

1. That coming to Jesus Christ aright is an effect of their being, of God, given to Christ before. Note, 'They shall

come.' Who? Those that are given. They come, then, because they were given, 'Thine they were, and thou gavest them me.' Now, this is indeed a singular comfort to them that are coming in truth to Christ, to think that the reason why they come is because they were given of the Father before to him. Thus, then, may the coming soul reason with itself as it comes. Am I coming, indeed, to Jesus Christ? This coming of mine is not to be attributed to me or to my goodness, but to the grace and gift of God to Christ. God gave first my person to him, and, therefore, has now given me a heart to come.

2. These words, *shall come*, make your coming not only the fruit of the gift of the Father, but also of the purpose of the Son; for these words are a Divine purpose; they show us the heavenly determination of the Son. 'The Father has given them to me, and they shall; yes, they shall come to me.' Christ is as full in his resolution to save those given to him as is the Father in the giving of them. Christ prizes the gift of his Father; he will lose nothing of it; he is resolved to save it every whit by his blood, and to raise it up again at the last day; and thus he fulfills his Father's will, and accomplishes his own desires (*John* 6:39).

3. These words, *shall come*, make your coming to be also the effect of an absolute promise. Coming sinner, you are concluded in a promise; your coming is the fruit of the faithfulness of an absolute promise. It was this

promise, by the virtue of which you at first received strength to come; and this is the promise, by the virtue of which you shall be effectually brought to him. It was said to Abraham, 'At this time will I come, and Sarah shall have a son.' This son was Isaac. Mark! 'Sarah shall have a son', there is the promise. And Sarah had a son; there was the fulfilling of the promise; and, therefore, was Isaac called the child of the promise (*Gen.* 17:19; 18:10; *Rom.* 9:9). Sarah shall have a son. But how, if Sarah be past age? Why, still the promise continues to say, Sarah shall have a son. But how, if Sarah be barren? Why, still the promise says, Sarah shall have a son. But Abraham's body is now dead. Why, the promise is still the same, Sarah shall have a son.

Thus, you see what virtue there is in an absolute promise. It carries enough in its own bowels to accomplish the thing promised, whether or not there are means in us to effect it. Therefore, this promise in the text, being an absolute promise, by virtue of it, not by virtue of ourselves, or by our own inducements, we come to Jesus Christ: for so are the words of the text: 'All that the Father giveth me shall come to me.'

Therefore is every sincere comer to Jesus Christ called also a child of the promise. 'Now we, brethren, as Isaac was, are the children of promise' (*Gal.* 4:28); that is, we are the children that God has promised to Jesus Christ, and given to him; yes, the children that Jesus Christ has promised shall come to him. 'All that the Father giveth me shall come.'

4. This word, *shall come*, engages Christ to communicate all manner of grace to those thus given him to make them effectually to come to him. 'They shall come'; that is, not if they will, but if grace, all grace, if power, wisdom, a new heart, and the Holy Spirit, and all joining together, can make them come. I say, this word, *shall come*, being absolute, has no dependence upon our own will, or power, or goodness; but it engages for us even God himself, Christ himself, the Spirit himself.

When God had made that absolute promise to Abraham, that Sarah 'should have a son', Abraham did not at all look at any qualification in himself, because the promise looked at none; but as God had, by the promise, absolutely promised him a son, so he considered now not his own body now dead, nor yet the barrenness of Sarah's womb. 'He staggered not at the promise of God through unbelief; but was strong in faith, giving glory to God; and being fully persuaded that what he had promised he was able also to perform' (*Rom.* 4:20–21).

He had promised, and had promised absolutely, Sarah shall have a son. Therefore, Abraham looks that he, namely, God, must fulfil the condition of it. Neither is this expectation of Abraham disapproved by the Holy Ghost, but accounted good and laudable; it being that by which he gave glory to God. The Father, also, has given to Christ a certain number of souls for him to save; and he himself has said, 'They shall come to me.' Let the church of God then live in a joyful expectation of the utmost accomplishment of this promise; for assuredly it shall be fulfilled, and not one thousandth part of a tittle thereof shall fail. 'They SHALL come to me.'

Secondly, *in particular.* And now, before I go any further, I will more particularly inquire into the nature of an absolute promise.

1. We call that an absolute promise that is made without any condition; or more fully thus: that is an absolute promise of God, or of Christ, which makes over to this or that man any saving, spiritual blessing, without a condition to be done on our part for the obtaining of it. And this we have in hand is such a one. Let the best Master of Arts on earth show me, if he can, any condition in this text depending upon any qualification in us which it is not, by the same promise, concluded, that it shall be, by the Lord Jesus, effected in us.

2. An absolute promise therefore is, as we say, without *if* or *and*; that is, it requires nothing of us, that itself might be accomplished. It says not, They shall, if they will; but, They shall. Not, They shall, if they use the means; but, They shall. You may say, that a will and the use of the means are supposed, though not expressed. But I answer, No, by no means; that is, as a condition of this promise. If they are at all included in the promise, they are included there as the fruit of the absolute promise, not as if it expected the qualification to arise from us. 'Thy people shall be willing in the day of thy power' (*Psa.* 110:3). That is another absolute promise. But does that promise

suppose a willingness in us, as a condition of God's making us willing? 'They shall be willing, if they are willing'; or, 'They shall be willing, if they will be willing.' This is ridiculous; there is nothing of this supposed. The promise is absolute as to us; all that it engages for its own accomplishment is the mighty power of Christ and his faithfulness to accomplish.

3. The difference, therefore, between the absolute and conditional promise is this:

i. They differ in their terms. The absolute promises say, 'I will, and you shall'; the other, 'I will, if you will'; or, 'Do this, and you shall live' (*Jer.* 4:1; 31:31–33; *Ezek.* 18:30–32; 36:24–34; *Heb.* 8:7–13; *Matt.* 19:21).

ii. They differ in their way of communicating good things to men; the absolute ones communicate things freely, only of grace; the other, if there be that qualification in us that the promise calls for, not otherwise.

iii. The absolute promises therefore engage God, the other engage us: I mean, God only, us only.

iv. Absolute promises must be fulfilled; conditional may or may not be fulfilled. The absolute ones must be fulfilled, because of the faithfulness of God; the other may not, because of the unfaithfulness of men.

v. Absolute promises have therefore a sufficiency in themselves to bring about their own fulfilling; the conditional have not so. The absolute promise is therefore a big-bellied promise, because it has in itself a fulness of all desired things for us; and will, when the time of that promise is come, yield to us mortals that which will verily save us; yes, and make us capable of answering the demands of the promise that is conditional.

4. Therefore, though there be a real, yes, an eternal difference, in these things and others, between the conditional and absolute promise, yet again, in other respects, there is a blessed harmony between them; as may be seen in these particulars. The conditional promise calls for repentance, the absolute promise gives it (*Acts* 5:31). The conditional promise calls for faith, the absolute promise gives it (*Zeph.* 3:12; *Rom.* 15:12). The conditional promise calls for a new heart, the absolute promise gives it (*Ezek.* 36:25–26). The conditional promise calls for holy obedience, the absolute promise gives it, or causes it (*Ezek.* 36:27).

5. And as they harmoniously agree in this, so again the conditional promise blesses the man who, by the absolute promise, is endued with its fruit. As, for instance, the absolute promise makes men upright; and then the conditional follows, saying, 'Blessed are the undefiled in the way, who walk in the law of the LORD' (*Psa.* 119:1). The absolute promise gives to this man the fear of the Lord;

and then the conditional follows, saying, 'Blessed is every one that feareth the LORD' (*Psa.* 128:1). The absolute promise gives faith, and then this conditional follows, saying, 'Blessed is she that believed' (*Zeph.* 3:12; *Luke* 1:45). The absolute promise brings free forgiveness of sins; and then says the condition, 'Blessed are they whose iniquities are forgiven, and whose sins are covered' (*Rom.* 4:7). The absolute promise says that God's elect shall hold out to the end; then the conditional follows with his blessings, 'He that shall endure unto the end, the same shall be saved' (*1 Pet.* 1:4–6; *Matt.* 24:13). Thus do the promises gloriously serve one another, and us, in this their harmonious agreement.

Now, the promise under consideration is an absolute promise. 'All that the Father giveth me shall come to me.' This promise therefore is, as is said, a big-bellied promise, and has in itself all those things to bestow upon us that the conditional calls for at our hands. *They shall come!* Shall they come? Yes, they shall come. But how, if they want those things, those graces, power and heart, without which they cannot come? Why, SHALL-COME answers all this, and all things else that may in this manner be objected. And here I will take the liberty to amplify things.

OBJECTIONS TO THE FORCE OF 'SHALL-COME' ANSWERED

OBJECTION 1: But they are dead, dead in trespasses and sins. How shall they then come?

ANSWER: Why, SHALL-COME can raise them from this death. 'The hour is coming, and now is, when the dead shall hear the voice of the Son of God, and they that hear shall live.' Thus, therefore, is this impediment by SHALL-COME removed out of the way. They shall be healed; they shall live.

OBJECTION 2: But they are Satan's captives; he takes them captive at his will, and he is stronger than they. How then can they come?

ANSWER: Why, SHALL-COME has also provided a help for this. Satan had bound that daughter of Abraham so, that she could by no means lift up herself; but yet SHALL-COME set her free both in body and soul. Christ will have them turned from the power of Satan to God. But what! Must it be, if they turn themselves, or do something to merit of him to turn them? No, he will do it freely, of his own good will. Alas! Man, whose soul is possessed by the devil, is turned whithersoever that governor lists, is taken captive by him, notwithstanding its natural powers, at his will; but what will he do? Will he hold him when SHALL-COME puts forth itself, will he then hinder him, for coming to Jesus Christ? No, that cannot be! His power is but the power of a fallen angel, but SHALL-COME is the Word of God. Therefore SHALL-COME must be fulfilled. 'And the gates of hell shall not prevail against it.'

There were seven devils in Mary Magdalene, too many for her to escape from under their power. But when the time was come that SHALL-COME was to be fulfilled upon her, they give place, fly from her, and she comes indeed to Jesus Christ, according as it is written, 'All that the Father giveth me shall come to me.'

The man that was possessed with a legion (*Mark* 5) was too much captivated by them for him by human force to come; yes, had he had, to boot, all the men under heaven to help him, had he that said, 'He shall come', withheld his mighty power. But when this promise was to be fulfilled upon him, then he comes; nor could all their power hinder his coming. It was also this SHALL-COME that preserved him from death; when by these evil spirits he was hurled hither and thither; and it was by the virtue of SHALL-COME that at last he was set at liberty from them, and enabled indeed to come to Christ. 'All that the Father giveth me shall come to me.'

OBJECTION 3: 'They shall', you say. But how if they will not? And, if so, then what can SHALL-COME do?

ANSWER: True, there are some men who say, 'We are lords; we will come no more unto you' (*Jer.* 2:31). But as God says in another case, If they are concerned in SHALL-COME to me, they 'shall know whose words shall stand, mine or theirs' (*Jer.* 44:28). Here, then, is the case. We must now see who will be the liar, he that saith, I will not; or he that saith, He shall come to me. You shall come, says God. I will not come, saith the sinner. Now, as sure as he is concerned in this SHALL-COME, God will make that man eat his own words, for *I will not* is the unadvised conclusion of a crazy-headed sinner. But SHALL-COME was spoken by him that is of power to perform his word. 'Son, go work to-day in my vineyard,' said the Father. But he answered, and said, I will not come. What now? Will he be able to stand to his refusal? Will he pursue his desperate denial? No, 'He afterwards repented and went.' But how came he by that repentance? Why, it was wrapped up for him in the absolute promise; and therefore, notwithstanding he said, 'I will not,' he afterwards repented and went.

By this parable Jesus Christ sets forth the obstinacy of the sinners of the world, as touching their coming to him; they will not come, though threatened: yes, though life be offered them upon condition of coming.

But now, when SHALL-COME, the absolute promise of God, comes to be fulfilled upon them, then they come; because by that promise a cure is provided against the rebellion of their wills. 'Thy people shall be willing in the day of thy power' (*Psa.* 110:3). Thy people, what people? Why, the people that your Father has given you. The obstinacy and plague that is in the will of that people shall be taken away; and they shall be made willing; SHALL-COME will make them willing to come.

He that had seen Paul in the midst of his outrages against Christ, his gospel, and people, would hardly have thought that he would ever have been a follower of Jesus Christ, especially since he went not against his conscience in his persecuting of them. He thought truly that he ought to do what he did. But we may see what SHALL-COME can do, when it comes to be fulfilled upon the soul of a rebellious sinner. He was a chosen vessel, given by the Father to the Son. And now, the time being come that SHALL-COME was to take him in hand, behold, he is over-mastered, astonished, and with trembling and reverence, in a moment becomes willing to be obedient to the heavenly call (*Acts* 9).

And were not they far gone that you read of (*Acts* 2), who had their hands and hearts in the murder of the Son of God, and to show their resolvedness never to repent of that horrid act, said, 'His blood be on us and on our children'? But must their obstinacy rule? Must they be bound to their own ruin, by the rebellion of their stubborn wills? No, not those of these the Father gave to Christ; therefore, at the times appointed, SHALL-COME breaks in among them; the absolute promise takes them in hand; and then they come indeed, crying out to Peter, and the rest of the apostles, 'Men and brethren, what shall we do?'

No stubbornness of man's will can stand, when God has absolutely said the contrary; SHALL-COME can make them come 'as doves to their windows' that had before resolved never to come to him.

The LORD spoke to Manasseh, and to his people, by the prophets, but would he hear? No, he would not. But shall Manasseh come off thus? No, he shall not. Therefore, he being also one of those whom the Father had given to the Son, and so falling within the bounds and reach of SHALL-COME, at last SHALL-COME takes him in hand, and then he comes indeed. He comes bowing and bending; he humbles himself greatly, and makes supplication to the LORD, and prays unto him; and he is entreated of him, and had mercy upon him (*2 Chron.* 30:10).

The thief upon the cross, at first, did rail with his fellow upon Jesus Christ; but he was one that the Father had given to him, and, therefore, SHALL-COME must handle him and his rebellious will. And behold, so soon as he is dealt with, by virtue of that absolute promise, how soon he buckles, leaves his railing, falls to supplicating of the Son of God for mercy; 'Lord,' says he, 'remember me when thou comest into thy kingdom' (*Matt.* 27:44; *Luke* 23:40–42).

OBJECTION 4: 'They shall come', say you, but how if they be blind, and see not the way? For some are kept off from Christ, not only by the obstinacy of their will, but by the blindness of their mind. Now, if they be blind, how shall they come?

ANSWER: The question is not, Are they blind? But, Are they within the reach and power of SHALL-COME? If so, that Christ who said, They shall come, will find them eyes, or a guide, or both, to bring them to himself. '*Must* is for the king.' If they shall come, they shall come. No impediment shall hinder. The Thessalonians' darkness did not hinder them from being the children of light. 'I am come,' said Christ, 'that they which see not might see.' And if he says, See, ye 'blind that have eyes,' who shall hinder it? (*Eph.* 5:8; *John* 9:39; *Isa.* 29:18; 43:8).

This promise, therefore, is, as I said, a big-bellied promise, having in the bowels of it, all things that shall occur to the complete fulfilling of itself. They shall come. But it is objected, that they are blind. Well, SHALL-COME is still the same, and continues to say, 'They shall come to me.' Therefore he says again, 'I will bring the blind by a way that they knew not, I will lead them in paths that they have not known; I will make darkness light before them, and crooked things straight. These things will I do unto them, and not forsake them' (*Isa.* 42:16).

Mark, I will bring them, though they be blind; I will bring them by a way they know not; 'I will . . . I will'; and therefore 'they shall come to me.'

OBJECTION 5: But how, if they have exceeded many in sin, and so made themselves far more abominable? They are the ringleading sinners in the county, the town, or family.

ANSWER: What then? Shall that hinder the execution of SHALL-COME? It is not transgressions, nor sins, nor all their transgressions in all their sins, if they by the Father are given to Christ to save them, that shall hinder this promise, that it should not be fulfilled upon them. 'In those days, and in that time,' says the LORD, 'the iniquity of Israel shall be sought for, and there shall be none; and the sins of Judah, and they shall not be found' (*Jer.* 50:20). Not that they had none, for they abounded in transgression (*2 Chron.* 33:9; *Ezek.* 16:48), but God would pardon, cover, hide, and put them away, by virtue of his absolute promise, by which they are given to Christ to save them. 'And I will cleanse them from all their iniquity, whereby they have sinned against me; and I will pardon all their iniquities, whereby they have transgressed against me. And it shall be to me a name of joy, a praise, and an honour before all the nations of the earth, which shall hear all the good that I do unto them; and they shall fear and tremble for all the goodness and for all the prosperity that I procure unto it' (*Jer.* 33:8–9).

OBJECTION 6: But how, if they have not faith and repentance? How shall they come then?

ANSWER: Why, he that says, *They shall come*, shall he not make it good? If they shall come, they shall come; and he that has said, they shall come, if faith and repentance be the way to come, as indeed they are, then faith and repentance shall be given to them! for SHALL-COME must be fulfilled on them.

1. *Faith shall be given them.* 'I will also leave in the midst of you an afflicted and poor people, and they shall trust in the name of the LORD.' 'There shall be a root of Jesse, and he that shall rise to reign over the Gentiles; in him shall the Gentiles trust' (*Zeph.* 3:12; *Rom.* 15:12).

2. *They shall have repentance.* He is exalted to give repentance. 'They shall come weeping, and seeking the LORD their God.' And again, 'With weeping and supplication will I lead them' (*Acts* 5:31; *Jer.* 31:9).

I told you before, that an absolute promise has all conditional ones in the belly of it, and also provision to answer all those qualifications, that they offer to him that seeks for their benefit. And it must be so; for if SHALL-COME be an absolute promise, as indeed it is, then it must be fulfilled upon every one of those concerned therein. I say, it must be fulfilled, if God can, by grace, and his absolute will, fulfil it. Besides, since coming and believing is all one, according to John 6:35, 'He that cometh to me shall never hunger, and he that believeth on me shall never thirst', then, when he says they shall come, it is as much as to say, they shall believe, and consequently repent, to the saving of the soul.

So then the present want of faith and repentance cannot make this promise of God of no effect; because this promise has in it to give what others call for and expect. *I will give them a heart, I will give them my Spirit, I will give them repentance, I will give them faith.* Mark these words: 'If any man be in Christ, he is a new creature.' But how came he to be a 'new creature', since none can create but God? Why, God indeed does make them 'new creatures'. 'Behold,' says he, 'I make all things new.' And hence it follows, even after he had said they are 'new creatures,' 'and all things are of God;' that is, all this new creation stands in the several operations, and special workings of the Spirit of grace, who is God (2 *Cor.* 5: 17–18).

OBJECTION 7: But how shall they escape all those dangerous and damnable opinions that, like rocks and quicksands, are in the way in which they are going?

ANSWER: Indeed this age is an age of errors, if ever there was an age of errors in the world; but yet the gift of the Father, laid claim to by the Son in the text, must needs escape these errors, and in conclusion come to him. There is a company of SHALL-COMES in the Bible that secures them; not but that they may be assaulted by them; yes, and also for a time entangled and detained by them from the Bishop of their souls. But these SHALL-COMES will break those chains and fetters that those given to Christ are entangled in, and they shall come, because he has said they shall come to him.

Indeed, errors are like that whore of whom you read in the Proverbs that sits in her seat in the high places of the city 'to call passengers who go right on their ways' (*Prov.* 9:13–16). But the persons, as I said, that by the Father are given to the Son to save them, are, at one time or other, secured by 'shall come to me'.

And therefore of such it is said, God will guide them *with his eye, with his counsels, by his Spirit, and that in the way of peace; by the springs of water, and into all truth* (*Psa.* 32:8; 73:24; *John* 16:13; *Luke* 1:79; *Isa.* 49:10). So then he that has such a guide, and all that the Father gives to Christ shall have it, he shall escape those dangers, he shall not err in the way. Yes, though he be a fool, he shall not err therein (*Isa.* 35:8), for of every such a one it is said, 'Thine ears shall hear a word behind thee, saying, This is the way, walk ye in it, when ye turn to the right hand, and when ye turn to the left' (*Isa.* 30:21).

There were thieves and robbers before Christ's coming, as there are also now; but, said he, 'The sheep did not hear them.' And why did they not hear them, but because they were under the power of SHALL-COME, that absolute promise, that had that grace in itself to bestow upon them, as could make them able rightly to distinguish of voices, 'My sheep hear my voice'? But how came they to hear it? Why, to them it is given to know and to hear, and that distinguishingly (*John* 10:8,16; 5:25; *Eph.* 5:14).

Further, the very plain sentence of the text makes provision against all these things. It says, 'All that the Father giveth me shall come to me;' that is, shall not be stopped, or be allured to take up anywhere short of ME, nor shall they turn aside, to abide with any besides ME.

4

Christ Receiving Sinners

'Him that cometh to me I will in no wise cast out'
(John 6:37).

'To me.' By these words there is further insinuated, though not expressed, a double cause of their coming to him. Firstly, there is in Christ a fulness of all-sufficiency of that, even of *all* that, which is needful to make us happy. Secondly, those that indeed come to him, do therefore come to him that they may receive it at his hand.

1. For the first of these, *there is in Christ a fulness of all-sufficiency of that, even of all that, which is needful to make us happy.*

Hence it is said, 'For it pleased the Father that in him should all fulness dwell' (*Col.* 1:19). And again, 'Of his fulness have all we received, and grace for grace' (*John* 1:16). It is also said of him that his riches are unsearchable, 'the unsearchable riches of Christ' (*Eph*. 3:8). Hear what he says of himself, 'Riches and honour are with me; yea, durable riches and righteousness. My fruit is better than gold, yea, than fine gold; and my revenue than choice silver. I lead in the way of righteousness, in the midst of the paths of judgment; that I may cause those that love me to inherit substance. And I will fill their treasures' (*Prov*. 8:18–21).

This in general. But, more particularly,

i. There is that *light* in Christ that is sufficient to lead them out of and from all that darkness, in the midst of which all others but them that come to him, stumble, and fall and perish. 'I am the light of the world,' says he, 'he that followeth me shall not walk in darkness, but shall have the light of life' (*John* 8:12). Man by nature is in darkness, and walks in darkness, and knows not where he goes, for darkness has blinded his eyes; neither can anything but Jesus Christ lead men out of this darkness. Natural conscience cannot do it; the ten commandments, though in the heart of man, cannot do it. This prerogative belongs only to Jesus Christ.

ii. There is that *life* in Christ, that is to be found nowhere else (*John* 5:40): life, as a principle in the soul, by which it shall be acted and enabled to do that which through Christ is pleasing to God. 'He that believeth in', or comes to, 'me,' says he, 'as the Scripture has said, out of his belly shall flow rivers of living water' (*John* 7:38). Without this life a man is dead, whether he be bad, or whether he be good; that is, good in his own, and other men's esteem. There is no true and eternal life but what is in the ME that speaks in the text.

There is also life for those that come to him, to be had by faith in his flesh and blood. 'He that eateth me, even he shall live by me' (*John* 6:57). And this is a life against that death that comes by the guilt of sin, and the curse of the law, under which all men are, and for ever must be, unless they eat the ME that speaks in the text. 'Whoso findeth ME,' says he, 'findeth life'; deliverance from that everlasting death and destruction, that, without me, he shall be devoured by (*Prov.* 8:35). Nothing is more desirable than life, to him that has in himself the sentence of condemnation; and here only is life to be found. This life, namely, eternal life, this life is in his Son (*1 John* 5:11); that is, in him that says in the text, 'All that the Father hath given me shall come to me.'

iii. The person speaking in the text is he alone by whom poor sinners have entrance to and acceptance with the Father, because of the glory of his *righteousness*, by and in which he presents them amiable and spotless in his sight. Neither is there any way besides him so to come to the Father: 'I am the way,' says he, 'the truth, and the life; no man cometh to the Father but by me' (*John* 14:6). All other ways to God are dead and damnable; the destroying cherubim stand with flaming swords, turning every way to keep all others from his presence (*Gen.* 3:24). I say, all others but them that come by him. 'I am the door; by me,' says he, 'if any man enter in, he shall be saved' (*John* 10:9).

The person speaking in the text is HE, and only HE, that can give stable and everlasting peace; therefore, says he, 'My peace I give unto you.' My peace, which is a peace with God, a peace of conscience, and of an everlasting duration. My peace, peace that cannot be matched, 'not as the world giveth, give I unto you'; for the world's peace is but carnal and transitory, but mine is divine and eternal. Hence it is called the peace of God, and it passeth all understanding.

iv. The person speaking in the text has enough of *all things truly spiritually good*, to satisfy the desires of every longing soul. 'Jesus stood and cried, saying, If any man thirst, let him come unto me, and drink.' And to him that is athirst, 'I will give of the fountain of the water of life freely' (*John* 7:37; *Rev.* 21:6).

v. With the person speaking in the text is *power* to perfect and defend, and deliver those that come to him for safeguard. 'All power', says he, 'is given unto me in heaven and in earth' (*Matt.* 28:18).

Thus might I multiply instances of this nature in abundance.

2. They that in truth do come to Christ do therefore come to him *that they might receive this fullness at his hand.*

They come for light, they come for life, they come for reconciliation with God; they also come for peace, they come that their soul may be satisfied with spiritual good, and that they may be protected by him against all spiritual and eternal damnation. And he alone is able to give them all this, to the filling of their joy to the full, as they also find when they come to him. This is evident:

i. From the plain declaration of those that already are come to him. 'Being justified by faith, we have peace with God through our Lord Jesus Christ, by whom also we have access by faith into this grace wherein we stand, and rejoice in hope of the glory of God' (*Rom.* 5:1–2).

ii. It is evident also, in that while they keep their eyes upon him, they never desire to change him for another, or to add to themselves some other thing, together with him, to make up their spiritual joy. 'God forbid', says Paul, 'that I should glory, save in the cross of our Lord Jesus Christ.' 'Yea, doubtless, and I count all things but loss for the excellency of the knowledge of Christ Jesus my Lord: for whom I have suffered the loss of all things, and do count them but dung, that I may win Christ, and be found in him, not having mine own righteousness, which is of the law, but that which is through the faith of Christ, the righteousness which is of God by faith' (*Phil.* 3:8–9).

iii. It is evident also, by their earnest desires that others might be made partakers of their blessedness. 'Brethren,' said Paul, 'my heart's desire and prayer to God for Israel is, that they might be saved.' That is, in that way that he expected to be saved himself. As he says also to the Galatians, 'Brethren,' says he, 'I beseech you, be as I am; for I am as ye are'; that is, I am a sinner as you are. Now, I beseech you, seek for life, as I am seeking of it; as if he was saying, 'For there is a sufficiency in the Lord Jesus both for me and you.'

iv. It is evident also, by the triumph that such men make over all their enemies, both bodily and spiritually: 'Now thanks be unto God,' said Paul, 'which always causeth us to triumph in Christ.' And, 'who shall separate us from the love of Christ,' our Lord? and again, 'O death, where is thy sting? O grave, where is thy victory? The sting of death is sin, and the strength of sin is the law; but thanks be to God, which giveth us the victory through our Lord Jesus Christ' (2 Cor. 2:14; Rom. 8:35; 1 Cor. 15:55–56).

v. It is evident also for that they are made by the glory of that which they have found in him, to suffer and endure what the devil and hell itself have or could invent, as a means to separate them from him. Again, 'Who shall separate us from the love of Christ? Shall tribulation, or distress, or persecution, or famine, or nakedness, or peril, or sword? As it is written, For thy sake we are killed all the day long, we are accounted as sheep for the slaughter.

Nay, in all these things we are more than conquerors, through him that loved us. For I am persuaded, that neither death, nor life, nor angels, nor principalities, nor powers, nor things present, nor things to come, nor height, nor depth, nor any other creature, shall be able to separate us from the love of God which is in Christ Jesus our Lord' (Rom. 8:35–39).

'Shall come TO ME.' Oh! the heart-attracting glory that is in Jesus Christ, when he is discovered, to draw those to him that are given to him of the Father; therefore those that came of old, rendered this as the cause of their coming to him: 'And we beheld his glory, the glory as of the only begotten of the Father' (*John* 1:14). And the reason why others come not, but perish in their sins, is for want of a sight of his glory. 'If our gospel be hid, it is hid to them that are lost: in whom the God of this world hath blinded the minds of them that believe not, lest the light of the glorious gospel of Christ, who is the image of God, should shine unto them' (2 *Cor.* 4:3–4).

There is therefore heart-pulling glory in Jesus Christ which, when discovered, draws the man to him; therefore, by 'shall come to me', Christ may mean, when his glory is discovered, then they must come, then they shall come to me. Therefore, as the true comers come with weeping and relenting, sensible of their own vileness, so again it is said that, 'the ransomed of the LORD shall return, and come to Zion with songs and everlasting joy upon their heads; they shall obtain joy and gladness, and sorrow and sighing shall flee away.' That is, at the sight of the glory of that grace that shows itself to them now in the face of our Lord Jesus Christ, and in the hopes that they now have of being with him in the heavenly tabernacles. Therefore it says again, 'With gladness and rejoicing shall they be brought; they shall enter into the King's palace' (*Isa.* 35:10; 51:11; *Psa.* 45:15). There is therefore heart-attracting glory in the Lord Jesus Christ which, when discovered, subjects the heart to the Word, and makes us come to him.

It is said of Abraham, that when he dwelt in Mesopotamia, 'the God of glory appeared unto him,' saying, 'Get thee out of thy country.' And what then? Why, away he went from his house and friends, and all the world could not stay him. Now, as the Psalmist says, 'Who is this King of glory?' he answers, 'The LORD, mighty in battle' (*Psa.* 24:8). And who was that, but he that 'spoiled principalities and powers,' when he did hang upon the tree, triumphing over them thereon? And who was that but Jesus Christ, even the person speaking in the text? Therefore he said of Abraham, 'He saw his day.' ' Yes,' says he to the Jews, 'your father Abraham rejoiced to see my day, and he saw it, and was glad' (*Col.* 2:15; *James* 2:23; *John* 8:56).

Indeed, the carnal man says, at least in his heart, 'There is no form or comeliness in Christ; and when we shall see him, there is no beauty that we should desire him' (*Isa.* 53:2); but he lies. This he speaks, as having never seen him. But they that stand in his house, and look upon him through the glass of his Word, by the help of his Holy Spirit, they will tell you other things. 'But we all,' say they, 'with open face, beholding as in a glass the glory of the Lord, are changed into the same image from glory to glory' (*2 Cor.* 3:18). They see glory in his person, glory in his undertakings, glory in the merit of his blood, and glory in the perfection of his righteousness; yes, heart-affecting, heart-sweetening, and heart-changing glory!

Indeed, his glory is veiled, and cannot be seen but as discovered by the Father (*Matt.* 11:27). It is veiled with flesh, with meanness of descent from the flesh, and with that ignominy and shame that attended him in the flesh. But they that can, in God's light, see through these things, they shall see glory in him; yes, such glory as will draw and pull their hearts to him.

Moses was the adopted son of Pharaoh's daughter; and for aught I know, had been king at last, had he now conformed to the present vanities that were there at court; but he could not, he would not do it. Why? What was the matter? Why! he saw more in the worst of Christ (bear with the expression), than he saw in the best of all the treasures of the land of Egypt. He 'refused to be called the son of Pharaoh's daughter; choosing rather to suffer affliction with the people of God, than to enjoy the pleasures of sin for a season; esteeming the reproach of Christ greater riches than the treasures in Egypt; for he had respect unto the recompence of the reward. He forsook Egypt, not fearing the wrath of the king.' But what emboldened him thus to do? Why, 'he endured', for he had a sight of the person speaking in the text. 'He endured, as seeing him who is invisible.' But I say, would a sight of Jesus have thus taken away Moses' heart from a crown, and a kingdom, etc., had he not by that sight seen more in him than was to be seen in them? (*Heb.* 11:24–26).

Therefore, when he says, 'shall come to me', he means they shall have a discovery of the glory of the grace that is in him. And the beauty and glory of that is of such virtue that it constrains, and forces, with a blessed violence, the hearts of those that are given to him.

Moses, of whom we spoke before, was no child when he was thus taken with the beauteous glory of his Lord. He was forty years old, and so consequently was able, being a man of that wisdom and opportunity as he was, to make the best judgment of the things, and of the goodness of them that was before him in the land of Egypt. But he, even he, was the one who set that low esteem upon the glory of Egypt as to count it not worth the meddling with, when he had a sight of this Lord Jesus Christ.

This wicked world thinks that the fancies of a heaven, and a happiness hereafter, may serve well enough to take the heart of such as either have not the world's good things to delight in, or that are fools, and know not how to delight themselves therein. But let them know again, that we have had men of all ranks and qualities that have been taken with the glory of our Lord Jesus, and have left all to follow him. As Abel, Seth, Enoch, Noah, Abraham, Isaac, Jacob, Moses, Samuel, David, Solomon; and who not, that had either wit or grace, to savour heavenly things? Indeed none can stand off from him, nor any longer hold out against him to whom he reveals the glory of his grace.

THE PROMISE TO THOSE COMING TO CHRIST

'And him that cometh to me I will in no wise cast out.' By these words our Lord Jesus sets forth yet more amply the great goodness of his nature towards the coming sinner. Before, he said, They shall come; and here he declares that *with heart and affections he will receive them*.

But, by the way, let me speak one word or two to the *seeming conditionality* of this promise with which now I have to do. It is evident, some may say, that Christ's receiving us to mercy depends upon our coming, and so our salvation by Christ is conditional. If we come, we shall be received; if not, we shall not; for that is fully intimated by the words. The promise of reception is only to him that comes: 'And him that cometh.'

I answer that the coming in these words mentioned, as a condition of being received to life, is that which is promised, yes, concluded to be effected in us, by the promise going before. In those latter words, coming to Christ is implicitly required of us; and in the words before, that grace that can make us come is positively promised to us. 'All that the Father giveth me shall come to me; and him that cometh to me I will in no wise cast out.' We come to Christ because it is said, We shall come; because it is given to us to come. So that the condition

[77]

which is expressed by Christ in these latter words is absolutely promised in the words before. And, indeed, the coming here intended is nothing else but the effect of 'shall come to me'. 'They shall come, and I will not cast them out.'

'*Him that cometh.*' He says not, 'him that is come', but 'him that comes'. To speak to these words, firstly, in general; and secondly, more particularly.

Firstly, in general. They suggest to us these four things:

1. That Jesus Christ does build upon it that, *since the Father gave his people to him, they shall be enabled to come to him.* 'And him that cometh.' As if he was saying, I know that since they are given to me, they shall be enabled to come to me. He says not, *if* they come, or I suppose they will come; but, 'and him that cometh'. By these words, therefore, he shows us that he addresses himself to the receiving of them whom the Father gave to him to save. I say, he addresses himself, or prepares himself to receive them. By which, as I said, he concludes or builds upon it that they shall indeed come to him. He looks that the Father should bring them into his bosom, and so stands ready to embrace them.

2. Christ also suggests by these words that *he very well knows who are given to him*; not by their coming to him, but by their being given to him. 'All that the Father giveth me shall come to me; and him that cometh,' etc. This *him* he knows to be one of them that the Father has given him;

and, therefore, he receives him, even because the Father has given him to him. 'I know my sheep,' says he. Not only those that already have knowledge of him, but those, too, that yet are ignorant of him. 'Other sheep I have', said he, 'which are not of this fold' (*John* 10:16); not of the Jewish church, but those that lie in their sins, even the rude and barbarous Gentiles. Therefore, when Paul was afraid to stay at Corinth, from a supposition that some mischief might befall him there – 'Be not afraid,' said the Lord Jesus to him, 'but speak, and hold not your peace . . . for I have much people in this city' (*Acts* 18:9–10). The people that the Lord here speaks of were not at this time accounted his by reason of a work of conversion that already had passed upon them, but by virtue of the gift of the Father; for he had given them to him. Therefore Paul was to stay here, to speak the word of the Lord to them, that, by his speaking, the Holy Ghost might effectually work over their souls, causing them to come to him, who was also ready, with heart and soul, to receive them.

3. Christ, by these words, also suggests, that *no more come to him than, indeed, are given him of the Father.* For the *him* in this place is one of the *all* that was mentioned by Christ before. 'All that the Father giveth me shall come to me', and every *him* of that *all*, 'I will in no wise cast out.' This the apostle insinuates when he says, 'He gave some, apostles; and some, prophets; and some, evange-lists; and some, pastors and teachers; for the perfecting of the saints, for the work of the ministry, for the edifying of

the body of Christ; till we all come in the unity of the faith, and of the knowledge of the Son of God, unto a perfect man, unto the measure of the stature of the fulness of Christ' (*Eph.* 4:11–13).

Mark, as in the text, so here he speaks of *all*. 'Until we all come.' We all! All who? Doubtless, 'All that the Father giveth to Christ.' This is further insinuated, because he called this *all* the body of Christ: the measure of the stature of the fulness of Christ. By which he means the universal number given; to wit, the true elect church, which is said to be his body and fulness (*Eph.* 1:22–23).

4. Christ Jesus, by these words, further suggests that *he is well content with this gift of the Father to him.* 'All that the Father giveth me shall come to me; and him that cometh to me I will in no wise cast out.' I will heartily, willingly, and with great content of mind, receive him.

They show us, also, that Christ's love in receiving is as large as his Father's love in giving, and no larger. Hence, he thanks him for his gift, and also thanks him for hiding of him and his things from the rest of the wicked (*Matt.* 11:25; *Luke* 10:21).

Secondly, and more particularly, 'And HIM that cometh.' This word HIM: by it Christ looks back to the gift of the Father; not only in the lump and whole of the gift, but to the every *him* of that lump. As if he said, I do not only accept the gift of my Father in the general, but have a special regard to every one of them in particular; and will secure not only some, or the greatest part, but every *him*, every particle. Not a hoof of all shall be lost or left behind. And, indeed, in this he consents to his Father's will, which is that of all that he has given him, he should lose nothing (*John* 6:39).

'*And him.*' Christ Jesus, also, by his thus dividing the gift of his Father into *hims*, and by his speaking of them in the singular number, shows what a particular work shall be wrought in each one, at the time appointed of the Father. 'And it shall come to pass in that day,' says the prophet, 'that the LORD shall beat off from the channel of the river unto the stream of Egypt, and ye shall be gathered one by one, O ye children of Israel.' Here are the *hims*, one by one, to be gathered to him by the Father (*Isa.* 27:12).

He shows also hereby that no lineage, kindred, or relation, can at all be profited by any outward or carnal union with the person that the Father has given to Christ. It is only *him*, the given HIM, the coming him, that he intends absolutely to secure. Men make a great ado with the children of believers; and oh! the children of believers! But if the child of the believer is not the *him* concerned in this absolute promise, it is not these men's great cry, nor yet what the parent or child can do, that can interest him in this promise of the Lord Christ, this absolute promise.

'*And him.*' There are various sorts of persons that the Father has given to Jesus Christ. They are not all of one rank, of one quality; some are high, some are low; some are wise, some fools; some are more civil, and complying with the law; some more profane, and averse to him and his gospel. Now, since those that are given to him are, in some sense, so diverse; and since he still says, 'And him that cometh,' etc., he by that gives us to understand that he is not, as men, for picking and choosing, taking a best and leaving a worst, but he is for him that the Father has given him, and that comes to him. 'He shall not alter it, nor change it, a good for a bad, or a bad for a good,' (*Lev.* 27:10); but will take him as he is, and will save his soul.

There is many a sad wretch given by the Father to Jesus Christ; but not one of them all is despised or slighted by him. It is said of those that the Father has given to Christ that they have done worse than the heathen; that they were murderers, thieves, drunkards, unclean persons, and what not; but he has received them, washed them, and saved them. A fit emblem of this sort is that wretched example, mentioned in Ezekiel 16, that was cast out in a stinking condition, to the loathing of its person, in the day that it was born. A creature in such a wretched condition that no eye pitied, to do any of the things there mentioned to it, or to have compassion upon it; no eye but his that speaks in the text.

'*And him.*' Let him be as red as blood, let him be as red as crimson. Some men are blood-red sinners, crimson sinners, sinners of a double dye; dipped and dipped again, before they come to Jesus Christ. Are you who are reading these lines such a one? Speak out, man! Are you such a one? And are you now coming to Jesus Christ for the mercy of justification, that you might be made white in his blood, and be covered with his righteousness? Fear not; forasmuch as this your coming demonstrates that you are of the number of them that the Father has given to Christ; for he will in no wise cast you out. 'Come now,' says Christ, 'and let us reason together; though your sins be as scarlet, they shall be as white as snow; though they be red like crimson, they shall be as wool' (*Isa.* 1:18).

'*And him.*' There was many a strange HIM came to Jesus Christ, in the days of his flesh; but he received them all, without turning any away; speaking to them 'of the kingdom of God, and heal[ing] them that had need of healing' (*Luke* 9:11; 4:40). These words, '*And him*', are therefore words to be wondered at. That not one of them who, by virtue of the Father's gift and drawing, are coming to Jesus Christ, I say, that not one of them, whatever they have been, whatever they have done, should be rejected or set by, but admitted to a share in his saving grace.

It is said in Luke, that the people 'wondered at the gracious words which proceeded out of his mouth' (4:22). Now, this is one of his gracious words; these words are like drops of honey, as it is said, 'Pleasant words are as an honey-comb, sweet to the soul, and health to the bones' (*Prov.* 16:24). These are gracious words indeed, even as full as a faithful and merciful High Priest could speak them. Luther says, 'When Christ speaks, he has a mouth as wide as heaven and earth.' That is, to speak fully to the encouragement of every sinful *him* that is coming to Jesus

Christ. And that his word is certain, hear how he himself confirms it: 'Heaven and earth', says he, 'shall pass away; but my words shall not pass away' (*Isa.* 51:6; *Matt.* 24:35).

It is also confirmed by the testimony of the four evangelists, who gave faithful relation of his loving reception of all sorts of coming sinners, whether they were publicans, harlots, thieves, possessed of devils, lunatics, and what not (*Luke* 19:1–10; *Matt.* 21:31; *Luke* 15; 23:43; *Mark* 16:9; 5:1-9).

This, then, shows us: 1. The greatness of the merits of Christ. 2. The willingness of his heart to impute those merits for life to the great, if coming, sinners.

1. This shows us *the greatness of the merits of Christ;* for it must not be supposed, that his words are bigger than his worthiness. He is strong to execute his word. He can do, as well as speak. He can do exceeding abundantly more than we ask or think, even to the uttermost, and outside of his word (*Eph.* 3:20). Now, then, since he includes any coming *him*, it must be concluded that he can save to the uttermost sin, any coming *him*.

Do you think, I say, that the Lord Jesus did not think before he spoke? He speaks all in righteousness, and therefore by his word we are to judge how mighty he is to save (*Isa.* 63:1). He speaks in righteousness, in very faithfulness, when he began to build this blessed gospel-fabric, our text. It was for that he had first sat down, and counted the cost; and for that, he knew he was able to finish it! What, Lord, any *him*? Any *him* that cometh to thee? This is a Christ worth looking after, this is a Christ worth coming to!

This, then, should teach us diligently to consider the natural force of every word of God; and to judge of Christ's ability to save, not by our sins, or by our shallow apprehensions of his grace, but by his Word, which is the true measure of grace. And if we do not judge thus, we shall dishonour his grace, lose the benefit of his Word, and needlessly fright ourselves into many discouragements, though coming to Jesus Christ. *Him*, any *him* that comes, has sufficient from this word of Christ to feed himself with hopes of salvation. As you are therefore coming, oh, coming sinner, judge whether Christ can save you by the true sense of his words. Judge, coming sinner, of the efficacy of his blood, of the perfection of his righteousness, and of the prevalency of his intercession, by his Word. 'And him', says he, 'that cometh to me I will in no wise cast out.' 'In no wise,' that is, for no sin. Judge therefore by his Word, how able he is to save you. It is said of God's sayings to the children of Israel, 'There failed not aught of any good thing which the LORD had spoken unto the house of Israel; all came to pass' (*Josh*. 21:45). And again, 'Not one thing hath failed of all the good things which the LORD your God spake concerning you, all are come to pass unto you; and not one thing hath failed thereof' (*Josh*. 23:14).

Coming sinner, whatever promise you find in the Word of Christ, strain it as much as you can, so long as you do not corrupt it, and his blood and merits will answer all. Whatever the Word says, or any true consequence that is drawn from it, that we may boldly venture upon. As here in the text he says, 'And him that cometh', indefinitely, without the least intimation of the rejection of any, though never so great, if he be a coming sinner. Take it then for granted, that you, whoever you are, if coming, you are intended in these words; neither shall it injure Christ at all, if, as Benhadad's servants served Ahab, you shall catch him at his word.

'Now,' says the text, 'the man did diligently observe whether anything would come from him,' namely, any word of grace, 'and did hastily catch it.' And it happened that Ahab had called Benhadad his brother. The man replied, therefore, 'Thy brother Benhadad!' (*1 Kings* 20:33), catching him at his word. Sinner, coming sinner, serve Jesus Christ thus, and he will take it kindly at your hands. When he in his argument called the Canaanitish woman a dog, she caught him at it, and says, 'Truth, Lord; yet the dogs eat of the crumbs which fall from their master's table.' I say, she caught him thus in his words, and he took it kindly, saying, 'O woman, great is thy faith; be it unto thee even as thou wilt' (*Matt.* 15:28). Catch him, coming sinner, catch him in his words. Surely he will take it kindly, and will not be offended at you.

2. The other thing that I told you is evident in these words, is this: *The willingness of Christ's heart to impute his merits for life to the great, if coming, sinner.* 'And him

that cometh to me I will in no wise cast out.' The awakened coming sinner does not so easily question the power of Christ as his willingness to save him. 'Lord, if thou wilt, you canst,' said one (*Matt.* 8:2). He did not put the *if* upon his power, but upon his will. He concluded he could, but he was not as fully of persuasion that he would. But we have the same ground to believe he will, as we have to believe he can; and, indeed, the ground for both is the Word of God.

If he was not willing, why did he promise? Why did he say he would receive the coming sinner? Coming sinner, take notice of this; we are used to pleading practices with men, and why not with God likewise? I am sure we have no more ground for the one than the other; for we have to plead the promise of a faithful God. Jacob took him there: 'Thou saidst,' said he, 'I will surely do thee good' (*Gen.* 32:12). For, from this promise, he concluded that it followed in reason, 'He must be willing.'

The text also gives some ground for us to draw the same conclusion. 'And him that cometh to me I will in no wise cast out.' Here is his willingness asserted, as well as his power suggested. It is worth your observation that Abraham's faith considered rather God's power than his willingness; that is, he drew his conclusion, 'I shall have a child', from the power that was in God to fulfil the promise to him. For he concluded he was willing to give him one, else he would not have promised one. 'He staggered not at the promise of God through unbelief; but was strong in faith, giving glory to God; and being fully persuaded that what he had promised he was able also to perform' (*Rom.* 4:20–21). But was not his faith exercised, or tried, about his willingness too? No, there was no show of reason for that, because he had promised it. Indeed, had he not promised it, he might lawfully have doubted it; but since he had promised it, there was left no ground at all for doubting, because his willingness to give a son was demonstrated in his promising him a son.

These words, therefore, are sufficient ground to encourage any coming sinner that Christ is willing to the extent of his power to receive him; and since he has power also to do what he will, there is no ground at all left to the coming sinner any more to doubt; but to come in full hope of acceptance, and of being received to grace and mercy. 'And him that cometh.' He says not, 'and him that is come'; but, 'and him that comes'; that is, 'and him whose heart begins to move after me, who is leaving all for my sake; him who is looking out, who is on his journey to me'. We must, therefore, distinguish between coming, and having come to Jesus Christ. He that has come to him has attained of him more sensibly what he felt before that he wanted, compared to him who is but yet coming to him.

HOW THE MAN THAT HAS COME TO CHRIST BENEFITS

A man that *has come* to Christ has the advantage of him that *is but coming* to him; and that in seven things.

1. He that has come to Christ is *nearer to him* than he that is but coming to him; for he that is but coming to him is yet, in some sense, at a distance from him; as it is said of the coming prodigal, 'And while he was yet a great way off' (*Luke* 15:20). Now he that is nearer to him has the best sight of him; and so is able to make the best judgment of his wonderful grace and beauty, as God says, 'Let them come near, then let them speak' (*Isa.* 41:1). And as the apostle John says, 'And we have seen and do testify that the Father sent the Son to be the Saviour of the world' (*1 John* 4:14). He that has not yet come, though he is coming, is not fit, not being indeed capable, to make that judgment of the worth and glory of the grace of Christ as he is that has come to him, and has seen and beheld it. Therefore, sinner, suspend your judgment till you have come nearer.

2. He that has come to Christ has the advantage of him that is but coming in that he is *eased of his burden*; for he that is but coming is not eased of his burden (*Matt.* 11:28). He that has come has cast his burden upon the Lord. By faith he has seen himself released from it; but he that is but coming has it yet, as to sense and feeling, upon his own shoulders. 'Come unto me, all ye that labour and are heavy laden', implies that their burden, though they are coming, is yet upon them, and so will be till indeed they have come to him.

3. He that has come to Christ has the advantage of him that is but coming in this also, namely, *he has drunk of*

the sweet and soul refreshing water of life; but he that is but coming has not. 'If any man thirst, let him come unto me and drink' (*John* 7:37).

Mark, he must come to him before he drinks: according to that of the prophet, 'Ho! every one that thirsteth, come ye to the waters.' He drinks not as he *comes*, but when he *has come* to the waters (*Isa.* 55:1).

4. He that has come to Christ has the advantage of him that as yet is but coming in this also, namely, *he is not so terrified with the noise, and, as I may call it, hue and cry, which the avenger of blood makes at the heels of him that yet is but coming to him*. When the slayer was on his flight to the city of his refuge, he had the noise or fear of the avenger of blood at his heels; but when he was come to the city, and had entered it, that noise ceased.

Even so it is with him that is but coming to Jesus Christ, he hears many a dreadful sound in his ear; sounds of death and damnation, which he that has come is at present freed from. Therefore he says, 'Come, and I will give you rest.' And so he says again, 'We that have believed, do enter into rest,' as he said, etc. (*Heb.* 4:3).

5. He, therefore, that has come to Christ, is *not so subject to those dejections, and castings down, by reason of the rage and assaults of the evil one*, as is the man that is but coming to Jesus Christ, though he has temptations too. 'And as he was yet a coming, the devil threw him

down, and tare him' (*Luke* 9:42). For he has, though Satan still roars upon him, those experimental comforts and refreshments, namely, in his treasury, to present himself with, in times of temptation and conflict; which he that is but coming has not.

6. He that has come to Christ has the advantage of him that is but coming to him, in this also, namely, *he has upon him the wedding garment,* etc., but he that is coming has not. The prodigal, when coming home to his father, was clothed with nothing but rags, and was tormented with an empty belly; but when he had come, the best robe is brought out, also the gold ring, and the shoes, yes, they are put upon him, to his great rejoicing. The fatted calf was killed for him; the music was struck up to make him merry; and thus also the Father himself sang of him, 'This my son was dead, and is alive again; was lost and is found' (*Luke* 15:24).

7. In a word, he that has come to Christ, *his groans and tears, his doubts and fears, are turned into songs and praises;* for he has now received the atonement, and the earnest of his inheritance. But he that is still a coming, has not those praises nor songs of deliverance with him; nor has he as yet received the atonement and earnest of his inheritance, which is the sealing testimony of the Holy Ghost, through the sprinkling of the blood of Christ upon his conscience, for he is not come (*Rom.* 5:11; *Eph.* 1:13; *Heb.* 12:22–24).

THE MEANING OF THE WORD, 'COMETH'

'And him that COMETH.' There is further to be gathered from this word *cometh* these following particulars:

1. *That Jesus Christ has his eye upon, and takes notice of, the first moving of the heart of a sinner after himself.* Coming sinner, you cannot move with desires after Christ but he sees the working of those desires in your heart. 'All my desire,' said David, 'is before thee; and my groaning is not hid from thee' (*Psa.* 38:9). This he spoke as he was coming, after he had backslidden, to the Lord Jesus Christ. It is said of the prodigal, that while he was yet a great way off, his father saw him, had his eye upon him and his heart went out after him (*Luke* 15:20).

When Nathanael was come to Jesus Christ, the Lord said to them that stood before him, 'Behold an Israelite indeed, in whom is no guile.' But Nathanael answered him, 'Whence knowest thou me?' Jesus answered, 'Before that Philip called thee, when thou wast under the fig-tree, I saw thee.' There, I suppose, Nathanael was pouring out his soul to God for mercy, or that he would give him good understanding about the Messiah to come; and Jesus saw all the workings of his honest heart at that time (*John* 1:47–48).

Zaccheus also had some secret movings of heart, such as they were, towards Jesus Christ, when he ran before, and climbed up the tree to see him; and the Lord Jesus Christ had his eye upon him. Therefore, when he was come to the place, he looked up to him, and bade him come down, 'For today,' said he, 'I must abide at thy house', in order to the further completing of the work of grace in his soul (*Luke* 19:1-9). Remember this, coming sinner.

2. *As Jesus Christ has his eye upon, so he has his heart open to receive the coming sinner.* This is verified by the text: 'And him that cometh to me I will in no wise cast out.' This is also discovered by his preparing of the way, in his making of it as easy as may be to the coming sinner; which preparation is manifest by those blessed words, 'I will in no wise cast out'; of which I will say more when we come to the place. And, 'when he was yet a great way off, his father saw him, and had compassion, and ran, and fell on his neck, and kissed him' (*Luke* 15:20). All these expressions do strongly prove that the heart of Christ is open to receive the coming sinner.

3. *As Jesus Christ has his eye upon, and his heart open to receive, so he has resolved already that nothing shall alienate his heart from receiving the coming sinner.* No sins of the coming sinner, nor the length of the time that he has dwelt in them, shall by any means prevail with Jesus Christ to reject him. Coming sinner, you are coming to a loving Lord Jesus!

4. These words therefore are dropped from his blessed mouth, on purpose *that the coming sinner might take*

encouragement to continue on his journey, until he has come indeed to Jesus Christ.

It was doubtless a great encouragement to blind Bartimeus, that Jesus Christ stood still and called him, when he was crying, 'Jesus, thou Son of David, have mercy on me'; therefore, it is said, he cast away his garment, 'rose, and came to Jesus' (*Mark* 10:48–50). Now, if a call to come has such encouragement in it, what is a promise of receiving such, but an encouragement much more? And observe, though he had a call to come, yet not having a promise, his faith was forced to work upon a mere consequence, saying, He calls me; and surely since he calls me, he will grant me my desire.

Ah! but coming sinner, you have no need to go so far as to draw (in this matter) consequences, because you have plain promises: 'And him that cometh to me I will in no wise cast out.' Here is a full, plain promise, yes, all the encouragement one can desire; for, suppose you were allowed to make a promise yourself, and Christ should attest that he would fulfil it for the sinner that comes to him, could you make a better promise? Could you invent a more full, free, or larger promise? A promise that looks at the first moving of the heart after Jesus Christ? A promise that declares, yes, that engages Christ Jesus to open his heart to receive the coming sinner? Yes, further, a promise that demonstrates that the Lord Jesus is resolved freely to receive, and will in no wise cast out, nor means to reject, the soul of the coming sinner! For all this lies fully in this promise, and does naturally flow from it.

Here you need not make use of far-fetched consequences, nor strain your wits, to force encouraging
arguments from the text. Coming sinner, the words are
plain: 'And him that cometh to me I will in no wise cast
out.'

5

Returning Sinners Will
Not Be Cast Out

'And him that cometh to me I will in no wise cast out'
(John 6:37).

'And him that COMETH.' There are two sorts of
sinners that are coming to Jesus Christ. Firstly,
him that has never, until of late, at all begun to come.
Secondly, *him that came formerly, and after that went
back*; but has since reconsidered, and is now coming
again. Both these sorts of sinners are intended by the HIM
in the text, as is evident, because both are now the coming sinner. 'And him that cometh.'

1. *The newly-awakened comer.*
For the first of these: the sinner that has never, until of
late, begun to come, his way is easier. I do not say, more

plain and open to come to Christ than is the other – those last not having the clog of a guilty conscience for the sin of backsliding hanging at their heels. But all the encouragement of the gospel, with all the invitations it contains to coming sinners, are as free and as open to the one as to the other; so that they may with the same freedom and liberty, as from the Word, both alike claim interest in the promise. 'All things are ready'; all things for the coming backsliders, as well as for the others: 'Come to the wedding.' 'And let him that is athirst come' (*Matt.* 22:1–4; *Rev.* 22:17).

2. *The returning backslider.*

But having spoken to the first of these already, I shall here pass it by; and shall speak a word or two to him that is coming, after backsliding, to Jesus Christ for life. Your way, O sinner of a double dye, your way is open to come to Jesus Christ. I mean you, whose heart, after long backsliding, thinks of turning to him again. Your way, I say, is open to him, as is the way of the other sorts of comers; as appears by what follows:

i. *Because the text makes no exception against you.* It does not say, 'And any *him* but a backslider, any *him* but him.' The text does not thus object, but indefinitely opens wide its golden arms to every coming soul, without the least exception; therefore you may come. And take heed that you shut not that door against your soul by unbelief, which God has opened by his grace.

ii. No, the text is so far from excepting against your coming, that *it strongly suggests that you are one of the souls intended*, O coming backslider; otherwise what need would there be for that clause to have been so inserted, 'I will in no wise cast out'? As if it was said, 'Though those that come now are such as have formerly backslidden, I will 'in no wise' cast away the fornicator, the covetous, the railer, the drunkard, or other common sinners, nor yet the backslider.'

iii. That the backslider is intended is evident:

a. For that he is sent to *by name*, 'Go, tell his disciples and Peter' (*Mark* 16:7). 'But Peter was a godly man.' True, but he was also a backslider, yes, a desperate backslider: he had denied his Master once, twice, thrice, cursing and swearing that he knew him not. If this was not backsliding, if this was not a high and eminent backsliding, yes, a higher backsliding than you are capable of, I have thought amiss.

Again, when David had backslidden, and had committed adultery and murder in his backsliding, he must be sent to by name: 'And', says the text, 'the LORD sent Nathan unto David.' And he sent him to tell him, after he had brought him to unfeigned acknowledgment, 'The LORD hath also put away (or forgiven) thy sin' (2 *Sam.* 12:1, 13). This man also was far gone; he took a man's wife, and killed her husband, and endeavoured to cover all with wicked dissimulation. He did this, I say, after God had exalted him, and showed him great favour;

therefore his transgression was heightened also by the prophet with mighty aggravations; yet he was accepted, and that with gladness, at the first step he took in his returning to Christ. For the first step of the backslider's return is to say, sensibly and unfeignedly, 'I have sinned.' But he had no sooner said thus, but a pardon was produced, yes, thrust into his bosom: 'And Nathan said unto David, The LORD has also put away thy sin.'

b. As the person of the backslider is mentioned by name, *so also is his sin*, so that, if possible, your objections against your returning to Christ may be taken out of your way. I say, your sin also is mentioned by name, and mixed, as mentioned, with words of grace and favour: 'I will heal their backsliding, I will love them freely' (*Hos.* 14:4). What do you say now, backslider?

c. No, further, you are not only mentioned by name, and your sin by the nature of it, but *you yourself, a returning backslider, are put amongst God's Israel*, 'Return, you backsliding Israel, says the Lord; and I will not cause mine anger to fall upon you; for I am merciful, says the Lord, and I will not keep anger for ever' (*Jer.* 3:12); *among his children;* among his children to whom he is married. 'Turn, O backsliding children, for I am married unto you' (verse 14).

Yes, after all this, as if his heart was so full of grace for them that he was pressed until he had uttered it before them, he adds, 'Return, ye backsliding children, and I will heal your backslidings' (verse 22).

d. No, further, the Lord has considered that the shame of your sin has stopped your mouth, and made you almost a prayerless man; and therefore he says to you, 'Take with you words, and turn to the LORD: say unto him, Take away all iniquity, and receive us graciously.' See his grace, that he himself should put words of encouragement into the heart of a backslider; as he says in another place, 'I taught Ephraim to go, taking him by the arms.' This is teaching him to go indeed, to hold him up by the arms; by the chin, as we say (*Hos.* 14:2; 11:3).

From what has been said, I conclude, even as I said before, that the *him* in the text, 'and him that cometh', includes both these sorts of sinners, and therefore both should freely come.

QUESTION 1: 'But where does Jesus Christ, in all the Word of the New Testament, expressly speak to a returning backslider with words of grace and peace? For what you have urged as yet, from the New Testament, is nothing but consequences drawn from this text. Indeed it is a full text for carnal ignorant sinners that come, but to me, who am a backslider, it yields but little relief.'

ANSWER: How? Only little encouragement from the text, when it is said, 'I will in no wise cast out'! What more could have been said? What is here omitted that might have been inserted, to make the promise more full and free? No, take all the promises in the Bible, all the freest promises with all the variety of expressions of whatever nature or extent, and they can but amount to the expressions of this very promise, 'I will in no wise cast out.' 'I will *for nothing, by no means, upon no account, however they have sinned, however they have backslidden, however they have provoked*, cast out the coming sinner.'

QUESTION 2: But you say, 'Where does Jesus Christ, in all the words of the New Testament, speak to a returning backslider with words of grace and peace, that is, under the name of a backslider?'

ANSWER: Where there is such plenty of examples in receiving backsliders, there is the less need for express words to that intent; one promise, as the text is, with those examples that are annexed, are instead of many promises. And besides, I reckon that the act of receiving is of as much, if not of more, encouragement, than is a bare promise to receive. Receiving is as good as the promise, and the fulfilling of it too; so that in the Old Testament you have the promise, and in the New, the fulfilling of it; and that in various examples.

i. Peter denied his master, once, twice, thrice, and that with open oath; yet Christ receives him again without the least hesitation or stick. Yes, he slips, stumbles, falls again, in downright dissimulation, and that to the hurt and fall of many others; but none of this does Christ make a bar to his salvation, but receives him again at his return, as if he knew nothing of the fault (*Gal.* 2).

ii. The rest of the disciples, even all of them, did backslide and leave the Lord Jesus in his greatest straits. 'Then all the disciples forsook him and fled' (*Matt.* 26:56); they returned, as he had foretold, every one to his own, and left him alone. But this also he passes over as a very light matter. Not that it was so indeed in itself, but the abundance of grace that was in him did lightly roll it away. After his resurrection, when first he appeared to them, he gives them not the least check for their perfidious dealings with him, but salutes them with words of grace, saying, 'All hail! Be not afraid, peace be to you; all power in heaven and earth is given unto me.' True, he rebuked them for their unbelief, for which also you deserve the same. For it is unbelief that alone puts Christ and his benefits from us (*John* 16:52; *Matt.* 28:9–11; *Luke* 24:39; *Mark* 16:14).

iii. The man that after a large profession lay with his father's wife committed a high transgression, even such a one that at that day was not heard of, no, not among the Gentiles. Therefore this was a desperate backsliding; yet, at his return, he was received, and accepted again to mercy (*1 Cor.* 5:1–2; *2 Cor.* 2:6–8).

iv. The thief that stole was bidden to steal no more; not at all doubting but that Christ was ready to forgive him this act of backsliding (*Eph.* 4:28).

Now all these are examples, particular instances of Christ's readiness to receive the backsliders to mercy; and, observe it, examples and proofs that he has done so are, to our unbelieving hearts, stronger encouragements than bare promises that he will do so.

But again, the Lord Jesus has added to these, for the encouragement of returning backsliders, to come to him:

A call to come, and he will receive them (*Rev.* 2:1-5; 14-16; 20-22; 3:1-3; 15-22). Therefore New Testament backsliders have encouragement to come.

A declaration of readiness to receive them that come, as here in the text, and in many other places, is plain. Therefore, 'Set thee up waymarks, make thee high heaps,' of the golden grace of the gospel, 'set thine heart toward the highway, even the way which thou wentest,' when you did backslide; 'Turn again, O virgin of Israel, turn again to these thy cities' (*Jer.* 31:21).

'*And him that cometh.*' He says not, and him that talks, that professes, that makes a show, a noise, or the like; but, him that comes. Christ will take leave to judge who, among the many that make a noise, are those indeed that are coming to him. It is not him that says he comes, nor him of whom others affirm that he comes; but him that Christ himself shall say does come, that is concerned in this text.

When the woman that had the bloody issue came to him for cure, there were others as well as she, that made a great bustle about him, that touched, yes, thronged him. Ah, but Christ could distinguish this woman from them all; 'And he looked round about' upon them all, 'to see her that had done this thing' (*Mark* 5:25–32). He was not concerned with the thronging, or touchings of the rest; for theirs were but accidental, or, at best, void of that which made her touch acceptable. Therefore Christ must be judge who they be that in truth are coming to him. Every man's ways are right in his own eyes, 'but the LORD weigheth the spirits' (*Prov.* 16:2). Therefore, every one concerned must be certain of his coming to Jesus Christ; for as your coming is, so shall your salvation be. If you come indeed, your salvation shall be indeed; but if you come but in outward appearance, so shall your salvation be. But of coming, see before, as also afterwards, in the *use* and *application*.

THE IMPORTANCE OF THE WORDS, 'TO ME'

'And him that cometh TO ME.' These words *to me* are also well to be heeded; for by them, as he secures those that come to him, so also he shows himself unconcerned with those that in their coming rest short, to turn aside to others. For you must know that every one that comes, comes not to Jesus Christ.

Some that come, come to Moses and to his law, and there take up for life. With these Christ is not concerned; with these his promise has not to do. 'Christ is become of no effect unto you; whosoever of you are justified by the law, ye are fallen from grace' (*Gal.* 5:4).

Again, some that came, came no further than to gospel ordinances and there stayed; they came not through them to Christ; neither with these is he concerned; nor will their 'Lord, Lord,' avail them anything in the great and dismal day. A man may come to, and also go from the place and ordinances of worship, and yet not be remembered by Christ. 'So I saw the wicked buried,' said Solomon, 'who had come and gone from the place of the holy, and they were forgotten in the city where they had so done; this is also vanity' (*Eccles.* 8:10).

'*To me.*' These words, therefore, are by Jesus Christ very carefully put in, and serve for caution and encouragement; for caution, in case we stop anywhere short of Christ in our coming; and for encouragement to those that shall in their coming, come past all, till they come to Jesus Christ. 'And him that cometh to me I will in no wise cast out.'

Reader, if you love your soul, take this caution kindly at the hands of Jesus Christ. You see your sickness, your wound, your necessity of salvation. Well, go not to king Jareb, for he cannot heal you, nor cure you of your wound (*Hos.* 5:13). Take the caution, I say, lest Christ, instead of being a Saviour to you, becomes a lion, a young lion, to tear you, and go away (*Hos.* 5:14). There is a coming, but not to the Most High; there is a coming, but not with the whole heart, but as it were feignedly; therefore take the caution kindly (*Jer.* 3:10; *Hos.* 7:16).

'And him that cometh *to me*'; Christ as a Saviour will stand alone, because his own arm alone has brought salvation to him. He will not be joined with Moses, nor suffer John the Baptist to be tabernacled by him. I say they must vanish, for Christ will stand alone (*Luke* 9:28–36). Yes, God the Father will have it so; therefore they must be parted from him, and a voice from heaven must come to bid the disciples hear only the beloved Son. Christ will not suffer any law, ordinance, statute, or judgment, to be partners with him in the salvation of the sinner.

No, he says not, 'and him that cometh to my WORD'; but, 'and him that cometh to ME'. The words of Christ, even his most blessed and free promises, such as this in the text, are not the Saviour of the world; for that is Christ himself, Christ himself only. The promises, therefore, are but to encourage the coming sinner to come to Jesus Christ, and not to rest in them, short of salvation by him. 'And him that cometh TO ME.' The man, therefore, that comes aright, casts all things behind his back, and looks not at, nor has his expectations from anything, but the Son of God alone; as David said, 'My soul, wait thou only upon God; for my expectation is from him. He only is my rock, and my salvation; he is my defence; I shall not be moved' (*Psa.* 62:5–6). His eye is to Christ, his heart is to Christ, and his expectation is from him, from him only.

Therefore the man that comes to Christ, is one that has had deep considerations of his own sins, slighting thoughts of his own righteousness, and high thoughts of the blood and righteousness of Jesus Christ. Yes, he sees, as I have said, more virtue in the blood of Christ to save him, than there is in all his sins to damn him. He therefore sets Christ before his eyes; there is nothing in heaven or earth, he knows, that can save his soul and secure him from the wrath of God but Christ; that is, nothing but his personal righteousness and blood.

THE MEANING OF THE WORDS, 'IN NO WISE'

'And him that cometh to me, I will *in no wise* cast out.' IN NO WISE: by these words there is firstly, something expressed; and secondly, something implied.

1. That which is expressed is *Christ Jesus' unchangeable resolution to save the coming sinner*: 'I will in no wise reject him, or deny him the benefit of my death and right-eousness.' This word, therefore, is like that which he speaks of the everlasting damnation of the sinner in hell fire; 'He shall *by no means* depart thence', that is, never, never come out again, no, not to all eternity (*Matt.* 5:26; 25:46). So that as he that is condemned into hell fire has no ground of hope for his deliverance from there, so him that comes to Christ has no ground to fear he shall ever be cast in there.

'Thus says the LORD, If heaven above can be measured, and the foundations of the earth searched out beneath, I will also cast off all the seed of Israel, for all that they have done, says the Lord' (*Jer.* 31:37). 'Thus says the LORD, If my covenant be not with day and night, and if I have not appointed the ordinances of heaven and earth, then will I cast away the seed of Jacob' (*Jer.* 33:25–26). But heaven cannot be measured, nor the foundations of the earth searched out beneath. His covenant is also with day and night, and he has appointed the ordinances of heaven. Therefore he will not cast away the seed of Jacob, who are the coming ones, but will certainly save them from the dreadful wrath to come (*Jer.* 50:4–5).

By this, therefore, it is manifest, that it is not the greatness of sin, nor the long continuance in it, no, nor yet the backsliding, nor the pollution of your nature, that can put a bar in against, or be a hindrance of, the salvation of the coming sinner. For, if indeed this could be, then would this solemn and absolute determination of the Lord Jesus, of itself, fall to the ground, and be made of no effect. But his 'counsel shall stand, and he will do all his pleasure'; that is, his pleasure in this; for his promise, as to this irreversible conclusion, arises from his pleasure; he will stand to it, and will fulfil it, because it is his pleasure (*Isa.* 46:10–11).

Suppose that one man had the sins, or as many sins as a hundred men, and another should have a hundred times as many as he; yet, if they come, this word, 'I will in no wise cast out,' secures them both alike.

Suppose that a man has a desire to be saved, and for that purpose is coming in truth to Jesus Christ; but he, by his debauched life, has damned many in hell. Why, the door of hope is by these words set as open for him, as it is for him that has not the thousandth part of his transgressions. 'And him that cometh to me I will in no wise cast out.'

Suppose that a man is coming to Christ to be saved, and has nothing but sin, and an ill-spent life, to bring with him. Why, let him come, and welcome to Jesus Christ! He will frankly forgive him (*Luke* 7:42). Is not this love that passes knowledge? Is not this love the wonderment of angels? And is not this love worthy of all acceptation at the hands and hearts of all coming sinners?

2. That which is implied in the words is *the hindrances in coming to Christ.* i. The coming souls have those that continually lie at the feet of Jesus Christ to cast them off. ii. The coming souls are afraid that those will prevail with Christ to cast them off. For these words are spoken to satisfy us, and to stay up our spirits against these two dangers: 'I will in no wise cast out.'

i. *Coming souls have those that continually lie at the feet of Jesus Christ to cast them off.* And there are three things that thus bend themselves against the coming sinner.

a. There is *the devil,* that accuser of the brethren, that accuses them before God, day and night (*Rev.* 12:10). This prince of darkness is unwearied in this work; he does it, as you see, day and night; that is, without ceasing. He continually puts in his *caveats* against you, if so be he may prevail. How did he solicit importunately against that good man Job, if possibly he might have obtained his destruction in hell fire? He objected against him, that he served not God for nought, and tempted God to put forth his hand against him, urging, that if he did it, he would curse him to his face; and all this, as God witnesses, 'he did without a cause' (*Job* 1:9–11; 2:4–5). How did he solicit with Christ against Joshua the High Priest? 'And he showed me Joshua,' said the prophet, 'the high-priest, standing before the angel of the LORD, and Satan standing at his right hand to resist him' (*Zech.* 3:1).

To resist him: that is, to prevail with the Lord Jesus Christ to resist him; to object to the uncleanness and unlawful marriage of his sons with the Gentiles; for that was the crime that Satan laid against them (*Ezra* 10:18). Yes, and for all I know, Joshua was also guilty of the fact; but if not of that, of crimes no whit inferior; for he was clothed with filthy garments, as he stood before the angel. Neither had he one word to say in vindication of himself, against all that this wicked one had to say against him. But notwithstanding that, he came off well; but he might for it thank a good Lord Jesus, because he did not resist him, but to the contrary, took up his cause, pleaded against the devil, excusing his infirmity, and put justifying robes upon him before his adversary's face.

'And the LORD said unto Satan, The Lord rebuke thee, O Satan, even the LORD that has chosen Jerusalem, rebuke thee. Is not this a brand plucked out of the fire? And he answered and spoke to those that stood before him, saying, Take away the filthy garments from him; and unto him he said, Behold, I have caused thine iniquity to pass from thee, and I will clothe thee with change of raiment' (*Zech.* 3:2–4).

Again, how did Satan solicit against Peter, when he desired to have him, that he might sift him as wheat? That is, if possible, sever all grace from his heart, and leave him nothing but flesh and filth, to the end that he might make the Lord Jesus loathe and abhor him. 'Simon, Simon,' said Christ, 'Satan has desired to have you, that he may sift you as wheat.' But did he prevail against him? No: 'But I have prayed for thee, that thy faith fail not.' As if he said, Simon, Satan has desired me that I would give you up to him, and not only you, but all the rest of your brethren (for that is the meaning of the word 'you'), but I will not leave you in his hand. I have prayed for you. Your faith shall not fail; I will secure you to the heavenly inheritance (*Luke* 22:30–32).

b. As Satan, so *every sin of the coming sinner,* comes in with a voice against him, if perhaps they may prevail with Christ to cast off the soul. When Israel was coming out of Egypt to Canaan, how many times had their sins thrown them out of the mercy of God, had not Moses, as a type of Christ, stood in the breach to turn away his wrath from them (*Psa.* 106:23)! Our iniquities testify against us, and would certainly prevail against us, to our utter rejection and damnation, had we not an advocate with the Father, Jesus Christ the righteous (*1 John* 2:1–2).

The sins of the old world cried them down to hell; the sins of Sodom fetched upon them fire from heaven which devoured them; the sins of the Egyptians cried them down to hell, because they came not to Jesus Christ for life. Coming sinner, your sins are no whit less than any; no, perhaps, they are as big as all theirs. Why is it then that you live when they are dead, and that you have a promise of pardon when they had not? Why, you are coming to Jesus Christ, and therefore sin shall not be your ruin.

c. As Satan and sin, so *the law of Moses*, as it is a perfect holy law, has a voice against you before the face of God. 'There is one that accuseth you, even Moses,' his law (*John* 5:45). Yes, it accuses all men that have sinned against it of transgression; for as long as sin is sin, there will be a law to accuse for sin. But this accusation shall not prevail against the coming sinner; because it is Christ that died, and that ever lives, to make intercession for them that 'come to God by him' (*Rom.* 8; *Heb.* 7:25).

These things, I say, do accuse us before Christ Jesus; yes, and also to our own faces, if perhaps they might prevail against us. But these words, 'I will in no wise cast out', secure the coming sinner from them all.

The coming sinner is not saved because there is none that comes in against him, but because the Lord Jesus will not hear their accusations, will not cast out the coming sinner. When Shimei came down to meet king David, and to ask for pardon for his rebellion, up starts Abishai, and puts in his *caveat*, saying, Shall not Shimei die for this? This is the case of him that comes to Christ. He has this Abishai and that Abishai, that presently step in against him, saying, Shall not this rebel's sins destroy him in hell? Read further. But David answered, 'What have I to do with you, ye sons of Zeruiah, that ye should this day be adversaries unto me? Shall there any man be put to death this day in Israel, for do not I know, that I am king this day over Israel?' (*2 Sam.* 19:16–22). That is Christ's answer by the text, to all that accuse the coming *Shimeis*. What have I to do with you, that accuse the coming sinners to me? I count you adversaries that are against my showing mercy to them. Do not I know that I am exalted this day to be King of righteousness and King of peace? 'I will in no wise cast them out.'

ii. But again, these words do closely imply, *that the coming souls are afraid that these accusers will prevail against them*, as is evident, because the text is spoken for their relief and succour. That would not be needed if they that are coming were not subject to fear and despair on this account. Alas, there is guilt, and the curse lies upon the conscience of the coming sinner!

Besides, he is conscious to himself what a villain, what a wretch he has been against God and Christ. Also he now knows, by woeful experience, how he has been at Satan's beck, and at the motion of every lust. He has now also new thoughts of the holiness and justice of God. Also he feels that he cannot stop sinning against him. For the motions of sins, which are by the law, still work in his members, to bring forth fruit unto death (*Rom.* 7:5). But none of this needs to be a discouragement since we have so good, so tender-hearted, and so faithful a Jesus to come to, who will rather overthrow heaven and earth, than suffer a tittle of this text to fail. 'And him that cometh to me I will in no wise cast out.'

THE MEANING OF THE WORDS, 'TO CAST OUT'

Now, we have yet to inquire into two things that lie in the words, to which there has not yet been anything said. As, firstly, what it is to cast out; secondly, how it appears that Christ has power to save or cast out?

1. *What it is to cast out.*
To this I will speak, first, generally; second, more particularly. First, generally.

i. To cast out, is to slight and despise, and condemn; as it is said of Saul's shield, 'it was vilely cast away' (*2 Sam.* 1:21), that is, slighted and condemned. Thus it is with the sinners that come not to Jesus Christ. He slights, despises, and condemns them; that is, 'casts them away'.

ii. Things cast away are reputed as menstruous cloths, and as the dirt of the street (*Isa.* 3:24; *Psa.* 18:42; *Matt.* 5:13; 15:17). And thus it shall be with the men that come not to Jesus Christ, they shall be counted as menstruous, and as the dirt in the streets.

iii. To be cast out, or off, it is to be abhorred, not to be pitied, but to be put to perpetual shame (*Psa.* 44:9; 89:38; *Amos* 1:11).

But, secondly, more particularly, to come to the text. The casting out here mentioned is not limited to this or the other evil; therefore it must be extended to the most extreme and utmost misery. Or thus, he that comes to

Christ shall not lack anything that may make him evangelically happy in this world, or that which is to come; nor shall he that comes not lack anything that may make him spiritually and eternally miserable. But further, as it is to be generally taken with respect to *things that are now*, so also with respect to *things that shall be hereafter*.

i. As to *the things that are now*, they are either: a. More general, or b. More particular.

a. More general, thus:

(1) It is to be 'cast out' of the presence and favour of God. Thus was Cain cast out: 'Thou hast driven (or cast) me out this day . . . and from thy face', that is, from thy favour, 'shall I be hid.' A dreadful complaint! But the effect of a more dreadful judgment! (*Gen.* 4:14; *Jer.* 23:39; *1 Chron.* 28:9).

(2) To be 'cast out' is to be cast out of God's sight. God will look after them no more, care for them no more; nor will he watch over them any more for good (*2 Kings* 17:20; *Jer.* 7:15). Now they that are so, are left like blind men, to wander and fall into the pit of hell. This, therefore, is also a sad judgment! Therefore, here is the mercy of him that comes to Christ. He shall not be left to wander at uncertainties. The Lord Jesus Christ will keep him, as a shepherd does his sheep (*Psa.* 23). 'Him that cometh to me I will in no wise cast out.'

(3) To be 'cast out' is to be denied a place in God's house, and to be left as fugitives and vagabonds, to pass a little time away in this miserable life, and after that to go down to the dead (*Gal.* 4:30; *Gen.* 4:13–14; 21:10). Therefore here is the benefit of him that comes to Christ, he shall not be denied a place in God's house. They shall not be left like vagabonds in the world. 'Him that cometh to me I will in no wise cast out.' See Proverbs 14:26, Isaiah 56:3-5, Ephesians 1:19-22, 1 Corinthians 3:21-23.

(4) In a word, to be 'cast out' is to be rejected, as are the fallen angels. For their eternal damnation began at their being cast down from heaven to hell. So then, *not* to be cast out, is to have a place, a house, a habitation there; and to have a share in the privileges of elect angels.

These words, therefore, 'I will not cast out', will prove great words one day to them that come to Jesus Christ (*2 Pet.* 2:4; *John* 20:31; *Luke* 20:35).

b. Secondly, and more particularly:

(1) Christ has *everlasting life* for him that comes to him, and he shall never perish, for 'he will in no wise cast him out'; but for the rest, they are rejected, 'cast out', and must be damned (*John* 10:27–28).

(2) Christ has *everlasting righteousness* to clothe them with that come to him, and they shall be covered with it

as with a garment. But the rest shall be found in the filthy rags of their own stinking pollutions, and shall be wrapped up in them as in a winding-sheet, and so bear their shame before the Lord, and also before the angels (*Dan.* 9:27; *Isa.* 57:20; *Rev.* 3:4, 18; 16:15).

(3) Christ has *precious blood* that, like an open fountain, stands free for him to wash in, that comes to him for life, 'and he will in no wise cast him out'. But they that come not to him are rejected from a share in it, and are left to ireful vengeance for their sins (*Zech.* 13:1; *1 Pet.* 1:18–19; *John* 13:8; 3:16).

(4) Christ has *precious promises*, and they shall have a share in them that come to him for life; for 'he will in no wise cast them out'. But they that come not can have no share in them, because they are true only in him; for in him, and only in him, all the promises are Yea and Amen. Therefore they that come not to him are no whit the better for them (*Psa.* 50:16; *2 Cor.* 1:20–21).

(5) Christ has also *fulness of grace* in himself for them that come to him for life, 'and he will in no wise cast them out'. But those that come not to him are left in their graceless state; and as Christ leaves them, death, hell, and judgment find them. 'Whoso findeth me', says Christ, 'findeth life, and shall obtain favour of the Lord. But he that sinneth against me wrongeth his own soul: all they that hate me love death' (*Prov.* 8:35–36).

(6) Christ is *an Intercessor*, and ever lives to make intercession for them that come to God by him: 'But their sorrows shall be multiplied, that hasten after another', or other gods, their sins and lusts. 'Their drink-offerings will I not offer, nor take up their names into my lips' (*Psa.* 16:4; *Heb.* 7:25).

(7) Christ has *wonderful love, bowels, and compassions*, for those that come to him; for 'he will in no wise cast them out'. But the rest will find him a lion rampant; he will one day tear them all to pieces. 'Now consider this,' says he, 'ye that forget God, lest I tear you in pieces, and there be none to deliver' (*Psa.* 50:22).

(8) Christ is one, *by and for whose sake those that come to him have their persons and performances accepted of the Father*, 'and he will in no wise cast them out'. But the rest must fly to the rocks and mountains for shelter, but all in vain, to hide them from his face and wrath (*Rev.* 6:15–17).

ii. But again, these words, CAST OUT, have a special look to what will be hereafter, even at the day of judgment. For then, and not until then, will be the great anathema and casting out made manifest, even manifest by execution. Therefore we here speak of this under two heads. Firstly, of the *casting out itself*. Secondly, of *the place into which they shall be cast* that shall then be cast out.

First, the casting out itself stands in two things: a. In a *preparatory work*, and b. In the manner of *executing the act*.

a. The preparatory work involves these three things:

(1) It involves *the separation of those that have not come to him from them that have*, at that day. Or thus: At the day of the great casting out, those that have not NOW come to him shall be separated from them that have; for them that have 'he will not cast out'.

'When the Son of man shall come in his glory, and all the holy angels with him, then shall he sit upon the throne of his glory; and before him shall be gathered all nations, and he shall separate them one from another, as a shepherd divideth his sheep from the goats' (*Matt.* 25:31–32). This dreadful separation, therefore, shall then be made between them that NOW come to Christ and them that come not. And good reason; for since they would not with us come to him now they have time, why should they stand with us when judgment is come?

(2) They shall be *placed before him according to their condition*: they that have come to him, in great dignity, even at his right hand, for 'he will in no wise cast them out'. But the rest shall be set at his left hand, the place of disgrace and shame; for they did not come to him for life. They shall be distinguished also by fit terms: those that come to him he calls the *sheep*, but the rest are self-willed goats: 'And he shall separate them one from another, as a

shepherd divideth his sheep from the goats.' The sheep will be set on the right hand – next to heaven gate, for they came to him – but the goats on his left, to go from him into hell, because they are not of his sheep.

(3) Then will Christ proceed to the conviction of those that came not to him, and will say, 'I was a stranger, and ye took me not in,' or did not come to me. Their excuse of themselves he will slight as dirt, and proceed to their final judgment.

b. Now when these wretched rejectors of Christ shall thus be set before him in their sins and convicted, this is the preparatory work after which will follow *the manner of executing the act,* which will be done in the presence of all the holy angels, and in the presence of all them that in their lifetime came to him, by saying to them, 'Depart from me, ye cursed, into everlasting fire, prepared for the devil and his angels.' Annexed to it is the reason: for you were cruel to me and mine; particularly discovered in these words, 'For I was an hungred, and ye gave me no meat; I was thirsty, and ye gave me no drink; I was a stranger, and ye took me not in; naked, and ye clothed me not: sick, and in prison, and ye visited me not' (*Matt. 25:41–43*).

Secondly, it now remains that we speak of *the place into which these shall be cast,* which, in the general, you have heard already, namely, the fire prepared for the devil and his angels. But, in particular, it is thus described:

a. It is called *Tophet*: 'For Tophet is ordained of old, yea, for the king', the Lucifer, 'it is prepared; he has made it deep and large; the pile thereof is fire and much wood; the breath of the LORD, like a stream of brimstone, doth kindle it' (*Isa.* 30:32).

b. It is called *hell*. 'It is better for thee to enter halt (lame) into life, than having two feet to be cast into hell' (*Mark* 9:45).

c. It is called *the wine press of the wrath of God*. 'And the angel thrust in his sickle into the earth, and gathered the vine of the earth,' that is, them that did not come to Christ, 'and cast it into the great wine-press of the wrath of God' (*Rev.* 14:19).

d. It is called *a lake of fire*. 'And whosoever was not found written in the book of life was cast into the lake of fire' (*Rev.* 20:15).

e. It is called *a pit*. 'Thou hast said in thine heart, I will ascend into heaven, I will exalt my throne above the stars of God: I will sit also upon the mount of the congregation, in the sides of the north . . . Yet thou shalt be brought down to hell, to the sides of the pit' (*Isa.* 14:13, 15).

f. It is called *a bottomless pit*, out of which the smoke and the locust came, and into which the great dragon was cast. And it is called *bottomless* to show the endlessness of the fall that they will have into it that come not, in the acceptable time, to Jesus Christ (*Rev.* 9:1–2; 20:3).

g. It is called *outer darkness*. 'Bind him hand and foot . . . and cast him into outer darkness', 'and cast ye the unprofitable servant into outer darkness', 'there shall be weeping and gnashing of teeth' (*Matt.* 22:13; 25:30).

h. It is called *a furnace of fire*. 'As therefore the tares are gathered and burned in the fire; so shall it be in the end of this world. The Son of man shall send forth his angels, and they shall gather out of his kingdom all things that offend, and them which do iniquity; and shall cast them into a furnace of fire: there shall be wailing and gnashing of teeth.' And again, 'So shall it be at the end of the world: the angels shall come forth, and sever the wicked from among the just, and shall cast them into the furnace of fire: there shall be wailing and gnashing of teeth' (*Matt.* 13:40–51).

Lastly, It may not be amiss, if, in the conclusion of this, I show in few words *to what the things that torment them in this state are compared*. Indeed, some of them have been occasionally mentioned already; as that they are compared:

To *wood* that burns.
To *fire*.
To *fire and brimstone*.

It is compared to *a worm*, a gnawing worm, a never dying gnawing worm. They are cast into hell, 'where their worm dieth not' (*Mark* 9:44).

It is called *unquenchable fire*: 'He will gather his wheat into the garner; but he will burn up the chaff with unquenchable fire' (*Matt.* 3:12; *Luke* 3:17).

It is called *everlasting destruction*: 'The Lord Jesus shall be revealed from heaven with his mighty angels in flaming fire, taking vengeance on them that know not God, and that obey not the gospel of our Lord Jesus Christ; who shall be punished with everlasting destruction from the presence of the Lord, and from the glory of his power' (*2 Thess.* 1:7–9).

It is called *wrath without mixture*, and is given them in the cup of his indignation. 'If any man worship the beast, and his image, and receive his mark in his forehead, or in his hand, the same shall drink of the wine of the wrath of God, which is poured out without mixture, into the cup of his indignation; and he shall be tormented with fire and brimstone in the presence of the holy angels, and in the presence of the Lamb' (*Rev.* 14:9–10).

It is called *the second death*. 'And death and hell were cast into the lake of fire. This is the second death. Blessed and holy is he that has part in the first resurrection: on such the second death hath no power' (*Rev.* 20:6, 14).

It is called *eternal damnation*. 'But he that shall blaspheme against the Holy Ghost, hath never forgiveness, but is in danger of eternal damnation.' Oh! these three words! Everlasting punishment! Eternal damnation! And

For ever and ever! How will they gnaw and eat up all the expectation of the end of the misery of the cast-away sinners. 'And the smoke of their torment ascendeth up for ever and ever; and they have no rest day nor night,' etc. (*Rev.* 14:11).

Their behaviour in hell is set forth by four things that I know of:

By *calling for help* and relief in vain;

By *weeping*;

By *wailing*;

By *gnashing of teeth*.

2. *The Power of Christ to Save or Cast Out*

And now we come to the second thing that is to be inquired into, namely, how it appears that Christ has power to save, or to cast out. For by these words, 'I will in no wise cast out', he declares that he has power to do both. Now this inquiry allows us to search into two things: First, how it appears that he has power to save; Second, how it appears that he has power to cast out.

First, that he has *power to save* appears by that which follows:

i. To speak only of Christ as he is Mediator: he was authorized to this blessed work by his Father, before the world began. Hence the apostle says, 'He has chosen us in him before the foundation of the world' (*Eph.* 1:4). With all those things that effectually will produce our salvation. Read the same chapter, with 2 Timothy 1:9.

ii. He was promised to our first parents, that he should, in the fulness of time, bruise the serpent's head; and, as Paul expounds it, redeem them that were under the law. Hence, since that time, he has been reckoned as slain for our sins. By which means all the fathers under the first testament were secured from the wrath to come; hence he is called, 'The Lamb slain from the foundation of the world' (*Rev.* 13:8; *Gen.* 3:15; *Gal.* 4:4–5).

iii. Moses gave testimony of him by the types and shadows, and bloody sacrifices, that he commanded from the mouth of God to be in use for the support of his people's faith, until the time of reformation, which was the time of the death of Jesus (See Hebrews chapters 9 and 10).

iv. At the time of his birth it was testified of him by the angel that he should 'save his people from their sins' (*Matt.* 1:21).

v. It is testified of him in the days of his flesh that he had power on earth to forgive sins (*Mark* 2:5–12).

vi. It is testified also of him by the apostle Peter that 'God hath exalted him with his own right hand, to be a prince and a Saviour, for to give repentance to Israel, and forgiveness of sins' (*Acts* 5:31).

vii. In a word, this is everywhere testified of him, both in the Old Testament and the New. With good reason he should be acknowledged and trusted in as a Saviour:

a. He came down from heaven to be a Saviour (*John* 6:38–40).

b. He was anointed when on earth to be a Saviour (*Luke* 3:22).

c. He did the works of a Saviour, as

He fulfilled the law, and became the end of it for righteousness, for them that believe in him (*Rom.* 10:3,4).

He laid down his life as a Saviour; he gave his life as 'a ransom for many' (*Matt.* 20:28; *Mark* 10:45; *1 Tim.* 2:6).

He has abolished death; destroyed the devil; put away sin; got the keys of hell and death; is ascended into heaven; is there accepted of God and bidden to sit at the right hand as a Saviour; and all this because his sacrifice for sins pleased God (*2 Tim.* 1:10; *Heb.* 2:14–15; 10: 12–13; *Eph.* 4:7–8; *John* 16:10–11; *Acts* 5:30–31).

d. God has sent out and proclaimed him as a Saviour, and tells the world that we have redemption through his blood, that he will justify us, if we believe in his blood, and that he can faithfully and justly do it. Yes, God beseeches us to be reconciled to him by his Son; which could not be if he were not anointed by him to this very purpose, and also if his works and undertakings considered as a Saviour were not accepted of God (*Rom.* 3:24–25; *2 Cor.* 5:18–21).

e. God has received already millions of souls into his paradise, because they have received this Jesus for a

Saviour; and is resolved to cut them off, and to cast them out of his presence, that will not take him for a Saviour (*Heb.* 12:22–26).

I intend brevity here; therefore a word concerning the second, and then to conclude.

Secondly, how it appears that he has *power to cast out*. This appears also by what follows:

i. The Father, for the service that he has done him as Saviour, has made him Lord of all, even Lord of quick and dead. 'For to this end Christ both died, and rose, and revived, that he might be Lord both of the dead and living' (*Rom.* 14:9).

ii. The Father has left it with him to quicken whom he will, namely, with saving grace, and to cast out whom he will, for their rebellion against him (*John* 5:21).

iii. The Father has made him judge of quick and dead, has committed all judgment unto the Son, and appointed that all should honour the Son, even as they honour the Father (*John* 5:22–23).

iv. God will judge the world by this man: the day is appointed for judgment, and he is appointed for judge. 'He has appointed a day in the which he will judge the world in righteousness by that man' (*Acts* 17:31). Therefore we must all appear before the judgment seat of Christ, that every one may receive for the things done in the body, according to what they have done. If they have closed with him, heaven and salvation; if they have not, hell and damnation! And for these reasons he must be Judge:

a. Because of his humiliation, because of his Father's word he humbled himself, and he became obedient unto death, even the death of the cross. 'Therefore God also hath highly exalted him, and given him a name which is above every name: that at the name of Jesus every knee should bow, of things in heaven, and things in earth, and things under the earth; and that every tongue should confess that Jesus Christ is Lord, to the glory of God the Father.' This has respect to his being Judge, and his sitting in judgment upon angels and men (*Phil.* 2:7–11; *Rom.* 14:10–11).

b. That all men might honour the Son, even as they honour the Father. 'For the Father judgeth no man, but has committed all judgment unto the Son; that all men should honour the Son, even as they honour the Father' (*John* 5:22–23).

c. Because of his righteous judgment, this work is fit for no creature; it is only fit for the Son of God. For he will reward every man according to his ways (*Rev.* 22:12).

d. Because he is the Son of man. He 'has given him authority to execute judgment also, because he is the Son of man' (*John* 5:27).

6

The Father Draws
Us to Christ

'*All that the Father giveth me shall come to me*'
(John 6:37).

Thus have I in brief passed through this text by way of *explanation*. My next work is to speak of it by way of *observation*. But I shall be also as brief in that as the nature of the thing will admit. 'All that the Father giveth me shall come to me; and him that cometh to me I will in no wise cast out' (*John* 6:37).

And now I come to some observations, and a little briefly to speak of them, and then conclude the whole. The words thus explained afford us many observations, some of which are these:

1. That God the Father, and Christ his Son, are two distinct Persons in the Godhead.

2. That by them, not excluding the Holy Ghost, is contrived and determined the salvation of fallen mankind.

3. That this contrivance resolved itself into a covenant between these Persons in the Godhead, which involves giving on the Father's part, and receiving on the Son's. 'All that the Father giveth me,' etc.

4. That every one that the Father has given to Christ, according to the mind of God in the text, shall certainly come to him.

5. That coming to Jesus Christ is therefore not by the will, wisdom, or power of man; but by the gift, promise, and drawing of the Father. 'All that the Father giveth me shall come.'

6. That Jesus Christ will be careful to receive, and will not in any wise reject those that come, or are coming to him: 'And him that cometh to me I will in no wise cast out.'

There are, besides these, some other truths implied in the words, such as:

7. They that are coming to Jesus Christ are often heartily afraid that he will not receive them.

8. Jesus Christ would not have them that in truth are coming to him once think that he will cast them out.

These observations lie all of them in the words, and are plentifully confirmed by the Scriptures of truth. But I shall not at this time speak of them all, but shall pass by the first, second, third, fourth, and sixth, partly because I design to be brief, and partly because they are touched upon in the explicatory part of the text. I shall therefore begin with the fifth observation, and so make that the first in order, in the following discourse.

OBSERVATION 1

First, then, *coming to Christ is not by the will, wisdom, or power of man, but by the gift, promise, and drawing of the Father.*

This observation involves two parts. Firstly, coming to Christ *is not by the will, wisdom, or power of man;* secondly, it *is by the gift, promise, and drawing of the Father.* That the text carries this truth in its bosom, you will find if you look into the previous explanation of the first part. I shall, therefore, here follow the method propounded, namely, to show:

1. *That coming to Christ is not by the will, wisdom, or power of man.* This is true because the Word does positively say it is not.

i. It denies it wholly to be by the *will* of man. 'Not of blood, nor of the will of the flesh, nor of the will of man' (*John* 1:13). And again, 'It is not of him that willeth, nor of him that runneth' (*Rom* 9:16).

ii. It denies it to be of the *wisdom* of man, as is manifest from these considerations:

a. In the wisdom of God it pleased him, that the world by wisdom should not know him. Now, if by their wisdom they cannot know him it follows that, by that wisdom, they cannot come unto him; for coming to him is not before but after some knowledge of him (*1 Cor.* 1:21; *Acts* 13:27; *Psa.* 9:10).

b. The wisdom of man, in God's account, as to the knowledge of Christ, is reckoned foolishness. 'Has not God made foolish the wisdom of this world?' (*1 Cor.* 1:20). And again, 'The wisdom of this world is foolishness with God' (*1 Cor.* 2:14). If God has made foolish the wisdom of this world; and again, if the wisdom of this world is foolishness with him, then truly it is not likely that by that a sinner should become so prudent as to come to Jesus Christ, especially if you consider:

c. That the doctrine of a crucified Christ, and so of salvation by him, is the very thing that is counted foolishness by the wisdom of the world. Now, if the very doctrine of a crucified Christ be counted foolishness by the wisdom of this world, it cannot be that, by that wisdom, a man should be drawn out in his soul to come to him (*1 Cor.* 3:19; 1:18, 23).

d. God counted the wisdom of this world one of his greatest enemies; therefore, by that wisdom no man can come to Jesus Christ. For it is not likely that one of God's greatest enemies should draw a man to that which best of all pleases God, as coming to Christ does. Now, that God counts the wisdom of this world one of his greatest enemies, is evident:

(1) In that it casts the greatest contempt upon his Son's undertakings, as was proved before, in that it counts his crucifixion foolishness; though that be one of the highest demonstrations of divine wisdom (*Eph.* 1:7–8).

(2) Because God has threatened to destroy it, and bring it to nought, and cause it to perish; which surely he would not do, were it not an enemy, and if it would direct men to, and cause them to close with Jesus Christ (*Isa.* 29:14; *1 Cor.* 1:19).

(3) He has rejected it from helping in the ministry of his Word, as a fruitless business, and a thing that comes to nought (*1 Cor.* 2:4, 6, 12, 13).

(4) Because it causes those that seek it and pursue it to perish (*1 Cor.* 1:18,19).

(5) And God has proclaimed that if any man will be wise in this world, he must be a fool in the wisdom of this world, and that is the way to be wise in the wisdom of God. 'If any man seemeth to be wise in this world, let him become a fool that he may be wise. For the wisdom of this world is foolishness with God' (*1 Cor.* 3:18–20).

iii. Coming to Christ is not by the *power* of man. This is evident partly:

a. From that which has gone before. For man's power in the putting forth of it, in this matter, is either stirred up by love, or by a sense of necessity; but the wisdom of this world neither gives man love to, nor sense of a need of, Jesus Christ; therefore, his power lies still.

And also from the following:

b. What power has he that is dead, as every natural man spiritually is, even dead in trespasses and sins? Dead, even as dead to God's New Testament things as he that is in his grave is dead to the things of this world. What power has he, then, by which to come to Jesus Christ? (*John* 5:25; *Eph.* 2:1; *Col.* 2:13).

c. God forbids the mighty man's glorying in his strength, and says positively, 'By strength shall no man prevail'; and again, 'Not by might, nor by power, but by my Spirit, saith the LORD' (*Jer.* 9:23–24; *1 Sam.* 2:9; *Zech.* 4:6; *1 Cor.* 1:27–31).

d. Paul acknowledges that man, even converted man, of himself has not a sufficiency of power in himself to think a good thought. If he cannot do that which is least – for to think is less than to come – then no man, by his own power, can come to Jesus Christ (*2 Cor.* 2:5).

e. Hence we are said to be made willing to come by the power of God; to be raised from a state of sin to a state of grace by the power of God; and to believe, that is, to come, through the exceeding working of his mighty power (*Psa.* 110:3; *Col.* 2:12; *Eph.* 1:18, 20; *Job* 23:14). But this power would not be needed, if man had either the power or the will to come, or so much as graciously to think of being willing to come, of himself to Jesus Christ.

2. I should now come to the proof of the second part of the observation namely, *that the coming to Christ is by the gift, promise, and drawing of the Father.*

But that is done already, in various parts of the explanation of the text, to which I refer the reader; for I shall here only give you a text or two more to the same purpose, and then come to the *use* and *application*.

i. It is expressly said, 'No man can come to me, except the Father which has sent me draw him' (*John* 6:44). By this text there is not only insinuated that in man is want of power, but also of will, to come to Jesus Christ: they must be drawn; they come not if they be not drawn. And observe, it is not man, no, nor all the angels in heaven, who can draw one sinner to Jesus Christ. 'No man comes to me, except the Father which has sent me draw him.'

ii. Again, 'No man can come unto me, except it were given unto him of my Father' (*John* 6:65). It is a heavenly gift that makes man come to Jesus Christ.

iii. Again, 'It is written in the prophets, And they shall be all taught of God. Every man, therefore, that has heard, and has learned of the Father, cometh unto me' (*John* 6:45).

I shall not enlarge, but shall make some *use* and *application*, and so come to the next observation.

USE AND APPLICATION OF OBSERVATION 1

FIRST USE: Is it so? Is coming to Jesus Christ not by the will, wisdom, or power of man, but by the gift, promise, and drawing of the Father? Then they are to blame that cry up the will, wisdom, and power of man, as things sufficient to bring men to Christ.

There are some men who think they may not be contradicted when they plead for the will, wisdom, and power of man in reference to the things that are of the kingdom of Christ. But I will say to such a man, he has never yet come to understand what the Scripture teaches concerning himself; nor has he ever known what coming to Christ is, by the teaching, gift, and drawing of the Father. He is such a one that has set up God's enemy in opposition to him, and that continues in such acts of defiance; and what his end, without a new birth, will be, the Scripture teaches also; but we will pass this.

SECOND USE: Is it so? Is coming to Jesus Christ by the gift, promise, and drawing of the Father? Then let saints here learn to ascribe their coming to Christ to the gift, promise, and drawing of the Father. Christian, bless God, who has given you to Jesus Christ by promise; and again, bless God for that he has drawn you to him. And why is it you? Why not another? Oh, that the glory of electing love should rest upon your head, and that the glory of the exceeding grace of God should take hold of your heart, and bring you to Jesus Christ!

THIRD USE: Is it so, that coming to Jesus Christ is by the Father, as said before? Then this should teach us to set a high esteem upon them that indeed are coming to Jesus Christ; I say, a high esteem on them, for the sake of him by virtue of whose grace they are made to come to Jesus Christ.

When men, by the help of human abilities, arrive at the knowledge of, and bring to pass that which, when done, is a wonder to the world, how he that did it is esteemed and commended! Yes, how are his wits, parts, industry, and unweariedness in all admired, and yet the man, as to this, is but of the world and his work the effect of natural ability; the things also attained by him end in vanity and vexation of spirit. Furthermore, perhaps in the pursuit of these his achievements, he sins against God, wastes his time vainly, and in the end loses his soul by neglecting better things; yet he is admired! But I say, if this man's parts, labour, diligence, and the like, will bring him to such applause and esteem in the world, what esteem should we have of such a one that is by the gift, promise, and power of God, coming to Jesus Christ?

1. *This is a man with whom God is*, in whom God works and walks; a man whose motion is governed and steered by the mighty hand of God, and the effectual working of his power. Here is a man!

2. *This man, by the power of God's might, which works in him, is able to cast a whole world behind him*, with all the lusts and pleasures of it, and to charge through all the

difficulties that men and devils can set against him. Here is a man!

3. *This man is travelling to Mount Zion*, the heavenly Jerusalem, the city of the living God, and to an innumerable company of angels, and the spirits of just men made perfect, to God the Judge of all, and to Jesus. Here is a man!

4. *This man can look upon death with comfort*, can laugh at destruction when it comes, and longs to hear the sound of the last trump, and to see his Judge coming in the clouds of heaven. Here is a man indeed!

Let Christians, then, esteem each other as such. I know you do it; but do it more and more. And that you may, consider these two or three things:

These are the objects of Christ's esteem (*Matt.* 12:48–49; 15:22–28; *Luke* 7:9).

These are the objects of the esteem of angels (*Dan.* 9:12; 10:21–22; 13:3–4; *Heb.* 2:14).

These have been the objects of the esteem of heathens, when but convinced about them (*Dan.* 5:10–11; *Acts* 5:15; *1 Cor.* 14:24–25). 'Let each [of you, then,] esteem [each] other better than themselves' (*Phil.* 2:2).

FOURTH USE: Again, is it so, that no man comes to Jesus Christ by the will, wisdom, and power of man, but by the gift, promise, and drawing of the Father? Then this shows us how horribly ignorant of this such are who make the man that is coming to Christ the object of their contempt and rage. These are also unreasonable and wicked men; men in whom is no faith (2 *Thess.* 3:2). Sinners, if you only knew what a blessed thing it is to come to Jesus Christ, and that it is by the help and drawing of the Father that they do indeed come to him. If you did, you would hang and burn in hell a thousand years, before you would turn your spirits, as you do, against him that God is drawing to Jesus Christ and also against the God that draws him.

But, faithless sinner, let us a little explore the matter. What has this man done against you, that is coming to Jesus Christ? Why do you make him the object of your scorn? Does his coming to Jesus Christ offend you? Does his pursuing of his own salvation offend you? Does his forsaking of his sins and pleasures offend you?

Poor coming man! 'Shall we sacrifice the abomination of the Egyptians before their eyes, and will they not stone us?' (*Exod.* 8:26).

But, I say, why are you offended at this? Is he ever the worse for coming to Jesus Christ, or for his loving and serving Jesus Christ? Or is he ever the more a fool, for flying from that which will drown you in hell fire, and for seeking eternal life? Besides, pray, Sirs, consider it; this he does, not of himself, but by the drawing of the Father. Come, let me tell you in your ear, you that will not come to him yourself, and him that would you hinder:

1. You shall be judged for one that has hated, maligned, and reproached Jesus Christ, to whom this poor sinner is coming.

2. You shall be judged, too, for one that has hated the Father, by whose powerful drawing this sinner does come.

3. You shall be taken and judged for one that has done despite to the Spirit of grace in him that is, by his help, coming to Jesus Christ. What do you say now? Will you stand by your actions? Will you continue to condemn and reproach the living God? Do you think that you shall weather it out well enough at the day of judgment? 'Can thine heart endure, or can thine hands be strong, in the days that I shall deal with thee?' says the LORD (*Ezek.* 22:14; *John* 15:18–25; *Jude* 15; *1 Thess.* 4:8).

FIFTH USE: Is it so, that no man comes to Jesus Christ by the will, wisdom, and power of man, but by the gift, promise, and drawing of the Father? Then this shows us how it comes to pass, that weak means are so powerful as to bring men out of their sins to a hearty pursuit after Jesus Christ.

When God, through Jethro, told Moses to speak to the people, he said, 'I will give you counsel, and God shall be with you' (*Exod.* 18:19). When God speaks, when God works, who can hinder it? None, none; then the work goes on! Elijah threw his mantle upon the shoulders of Elisha; and what a wonderful work followed! When Jesus fell in with the crowing of a cock, what work was there! Oh, when God is in the means, then shall that means – be it never so weak and contemptible in itself – work wonders (*1 Kings* 19:19; *Matt.* 26:74–75; *Mark* 14:71–72; *Luke* 22:60–62). The world understood not, nor believed, that the walls of Jericho should fall at the sound of rams' horns; but when God will work, the means must be effectual. A word weakly spoken, spoken with difficulty, in temptation, and in the midst of great contempt and scorn, works wonders, if the Lord your God will say so too.

SIXTH USE: Is it so? Does no man come to Jesus Christ by the will, wisdom, and power of man, but by the gift, promise, and drawing of the Father? Then here is room for Christians to stand and wonder at the effectual working of God's providences, that he has made use of as means to bring them to Jesus Christ.

For although men are drawn to Christ by the power of the Father, yet that power puts itself forth by the use of means; and these means are various, sometimes this, sometimes that; for God is at liberty to work by which, and when, and how he will. But let the means be what they will, and as contemptible as may be, yet God that commanded the light to shine out of darkness and that out of weakness can make strong, can, no, *does* often make use of very unlikely means to bring about the conversion and salvation of his people. Therefore, you that are come to Christ – and that by unlikely means – still yourselves, and wonder, and, wondering, magnify almighty power, by the work of which the means has been made effectual to bring you to Jesus Christ.

What was the providence that God made use of as a means, either more remote or more near, to bring you to Jesus Christ? Was it the removing of your habitation, the change of your condition, the loss of relations, estate, or the like? Was it your casting of your eye upon some good book, your hearing your neighbours talk of heavenly things, the beholding of God's judgments as executed upon others, or your own deliverance from them, or your being strangely placed under the ministry of some godly man? Oh, take notice of such providence or providences! They were sent and managed by mighty power to do you good. God himself, I say, has joined himself to this chariot. Yes, and so blessed it, that it failed not to accomplish the thing for which he sent it.

God does not bless to every one his providences in this manner. How many thousands are there in this world that pass every day under the same providences! But God is not in them, to do that work by them as he has done for your poor soul, by his effectually working with them. Oh, that Jesus Christ should meet you in this providence, that dispensation, or the other ordinance, this is grace indeed! This, therefore, it will be your wisdom to admire, and for this to bless God.

Give me leave to give you a taste of some of those providences that have been effectual, through the management of God, to bring salvation to the souls of his people.

1. The first shall be that of *the woman of Samaria*. It must happen that she must needs go out of the city to draw water, not before nor after, but just when Jesus Christ her Saviour was come from far, and set to rest himself, being weary, upon the well. What a blessed

providence was this, even a providence managed by almighty wisdom and almighty power, to the conversion and salvation of this poor creature! For by this providence was this poor creature and her Saviour brought together, that that blessed work might be fulfilled upon the woman, according to the purpose before determined by the Father (*John* 4).

2. What providence was it that there should be a tree in the way for Zaccheus to climb, thereby to give Jesus opportunity to call that chief of the publicans home to himself, even before he came down from it (*Luke* 19).

3. Was it not also wonderful that the thief of whom you read in the gospel should, by the providence of God, be cast into prison, to be condemned even at that session that Christ himself was to die? And that it should happen, too, that they must be hanged together, that the thief might be in hearing and observing of Jesus in his last words, that he might be converted by him before his death! (*Luke* 23).

4. What a strange providence it was, and as strangely managed by God, that Onesimus, when he had run away from his master, should be taken and, as I think, cast into that very prison where Paul lay bound for the Word of the gospel. That he might there be by him converted, and then sent home again to his master Philemon! Behold, 'All things work together for good to them that love God, to them who are the called according to his purpose' (*Rom.* 8:28).

I have myself known some that have been made to go to hear the Word preached against their wills; others have gone not to hear, but to see and to be seen; to jeer and flout others, as also to catch and carp at things. Some also to feed their adulterous eyes with the sight of beautiful objects; and yet God has made use even of these things, and even of the wicked and sinful proposals of sinners, to bring them under the grace that might save their souls.

SEVENTH USE: Does no man come to Jesus Christ but by the drawing of the Father? Then let me here caution those poor sinners, that are spectators of the change that God has wrought in them that are coming to Jesus Christ, not to attribute this work and change to other things and causes.

There are some poor sinners in the world that plainly see a change, a mighty change, in their neighbours and relations that are coming to Jesus Christ. But, as I said, they being ignorant and not knowing from where it comes and to where it goes, for 'so is every one that is born of the Spirit' (*John* 3:8), therefore they attribute this change to other causes: to melancholy; to sitting alone; to overmuch reading; to their going to too many sermons; to too much studying and musing on what they hear.

Also they conclude, on the other side, that it is for want of merry company; for want of medicine; and therefore they advise them to leave off reading, going to sermons, the company of sober people; and to be merry, to go a gossiping, to busy themselves in the things of this world, not to sit musing alone, etc. But come, poor ignorant sinner, let me deal with you. It seems you have become a counsellor for Satan. I tell you, you do not know what you are doing. Take heed of spending your judgment after this manner; you judge foolishly, and say in this, to every one that passes by, that you are a fool. What! Count convictions for sin, mournings for sin, and repentance for sin, melancholy? This is like those that on the other side said, 'These men are full of [drunk with] new wine.' Or as he that said Paul was mad (*Acts* 2:13; 26:24).

Poor ignorant sinner! Can you judge no better? What! Is sitting alone, pensive under God's hand, reading the Scriptures, and hearing sermons, etc., the way to be undone? The Lord open your eyes, and make you to see your error! You have set yourself against God, you have despised the operation of his hands, you attempt to murder souls. What! Can you give no better counsel touching those whom God has wounded than to send them to the ordinances of hell for help? You tell them to be merry and lightsome; but do you not know that 'the heart of fools is in the house of mirth?' (*Eccles.* 7:4).

You tell them to shun the hearing of thundering preachers; but is it not 'better to hear the rebuke of the wise, than for a man to hear the song of fools?' (*Eccles.* 7:5). You tell them to busy themselves in the things of this world; but do you not know that the Lord commands, 'Seek first the kingdom of God, and his righteousness?' (*Matt.* 6:33). Poor ignorant sinner! Hear the counsel of God to such, and learn yourself to be wiser. 'Is any afflicted? Let him pray. Is any merry? Let him sing psalms' (*James* 5:13). 'Blessed is the man that heareth me' (*Prov.* 8:34). And hear for time to come, 'Save yourselves from this untoward generation' (*Acts* 2:40). 'Search the Scriptures' (*John* 5:39). 'Give attendance to reading' (*1 Tim.* 4:13). 'It is better to go to the house of mourning' (*Eccles.* 7:2–3).

And will you judge him that acts in this way? You are almost like Elymas the sorcerer who sought to turn the deputy from the faith. You seek to pervert the right ways of the Lord. Take heed lest some heavy judgment overtake you (*Acts* 13:8–13). What! Teach men to quench convictions; take men off from a serious consideration of the evil of sin, of the terrors of the world to come, and how they shall escape the same? What! Teach men to put God and his Word out of their minds, by running to merry company, by running to the world, by gossiping? This is as much as to tell them to say to God, 'Depart from us, for we desire not the knowledge of thy ways;' or, 'What is the Almighty that we should serve him? Or what profit have we if we keep his ways?' Here is a devil in grain![1] What! Tell a man to walk 'according to the course of this world, according to the prince of the power of the air, the spirit that now worketh in the children of disobedience' (*Eph.* 2:2).

OBJECTION 1: 'But we do not know that such are coming to Jesus Christ; truly we wonder at them, and think they are fools.'

[1] Deeply engrained in the soul.

ANSWER: Do you not know that they are coming to Jesus Christ? Then they may be coming to him, for all that you know; and why will you be worse than the brute, to speak evil of the things you know not? What! Are you made to be taken and destroyed? Must you utterly perish in your own corruptions? (*2 Pet.* 2:12). Do you not know them? Let them alone then. If you cannot speak good of them, speak not bad. 'Refrain from these men, and let them alone; for if this counsel or this work be of men, it will come to nought; but if it be of God, ye cannot overthrow it, lest haply ye be found even to fight against God' (*Acts* 5:38,39).

But why do you wonder at a work of conviction and conversion? Do you not know that this is the judgment of God upon you, 'ye despisers, to behold, and wonder, and perish?' (*Acts* 13:40–41). But why wonder and think they are fools? Is the way of the just an abomination to you? See that passage, and be ashamed, 'He that is upright in the way is abomination to the wicked' (*Prov.* 29:27). Your wondering at them argues that you are strangers to yourselves, to conviction for sin, and to heartfelt desires to be saved; as also to coming to Jesus Christ.

OBJECTION 2: But how shall we know that such men are coming to Jesus Christ?

ANSWER: Who can make them see, whom Christ has made blind? (*John* 2:8–9). Nevertheless, because I endeavour your conviction, conversion, and salvation, consider. Do they cry because of sin, being burdened with it, as of an exceedingly bitter thing? Do they fly from it, as from the face of a deadly serpent? Do they cry because of the insufficiency of their own righteousness, as to justification in the sight of God? Do they cry out after the Lord Jesus, to save them? Do they see more worth and merit in one drop of Christ's blood to save them, than in all the sins of the world to damn them? Are they tender of sinning against Jesus Christ? Is his Name, Person, and undertakings, more precious to them, than is the glory of the world? Is this word more dear to them? Is faith in Christ (of which they are convinced by God's Spirit of the want of, and that without it they can never close with Christ) precious to them? Do they savour Christ in his Word, and do they leave all the world for his sake? And are they willing, God helping them, to run hazards for his name, for the love they bear to him? Are his saints precious to them?

If these things are so, whether you see them or not, these men are coming to Jesus Christ (*Rom.* 7:9–14; *Psa.* 38:3–8; *Heb.* 6:18–20; *Isa.* 64:6; *Phil.* 3:7–8; *Psa.* 54:1; 109:26; *Acts* 16:30; *Psa.* 51:7–8; *1 Pet.* 1:18–19; *Rom.* 7:24; *2 Cor.* 5:2; *Acts* 5:41; *James* 2:7; *Song of Sol.* 5:10–16; *Psa.* 119; *John* 13:35; *1 John* 4:7; 3:14; *John* 16:9; *Rom.* 14:23; *Heb.* 11:6; *Psa.* 19:10–11; *Jer.* 15:16; *Heb.* 11:24–27; *Acts* 20:22–24; 21:13; *Titus* 3:15; *2 John* 1; *Eph.* 4:16; *Philem.* 7; *1 Cor.* 16:24).

7

A Welcome for
Fearful Sinners

'Him that cometh to me I will in no wise cast out'
(John 6:37).

I come now to the second observation propounded to
be spoken to, namely, that *those that are coming to
Jesus Christ are often heartily afraid that Jesus Christ will
not receive them.*

I told you that this observation is implied in the text;
and I gather it:

Firstly, from the largeness and openness of the promise,
'I will in no wise cast out.' For had there not been a
proneness in us to fear 'casting out' Christ would not
have needed, as it were, to waylay our fear, as he does by
this great and strange expression, 'In no wise;' 'And him
that cometh to me I will in no wise cast out.' There would

not have been needed, as I might say, such a promise to be invented by the wisdom of heaven and worded in such a way, as if on purpose to dash in pieces at one blow all the objections of coming sinners, if they were not prone to admit of such objections, to the discouraging of their own souls. For this word, 'in no wise', cuts the throat of all objections; and it was dropped by the Lord Jesus with that very purpose and to help the faith that is mixed with unbelief. And it is, as it were, the sum of all promises; neither can any objection be made upon the unworthiness that you find in yourself, that this promise will not answer.

'But I am a great sinner', you say. 'I will in no wise cast out', says Christ.

'But I am an old sinner', you say. 'I will in no wise cast out', says Christ.

'But I am a hard-hearted sinner', you say. 'I will in no wise cast out', says Christ.

'But I am a backsliding sinner', you say. 'I will in no wise cast out', says Christ.

'But I have served Satan all my days', you say. 'I will in no wise cast out', says Christ.

'But I have sinned against light', you say. 'I will in no wise cast out', says Christ.

'But I have sinned against mercy', you say. 'I will in no wise cast out', says Christ.

'But I have no good thing to bring with me', you say. 'I will in no wise cast out', says Christ.

Thus I might go on to the end of things, and show you that still this promise was provided to answer all objections, and does answer them. But I say, what need is there of it, if they that are coming to Jesus Christ are not sometimes, yes, often, heartily afraid, that Jesus Christ will 'cast them out'?

Secondly, I will give you now two instances that seem to imply the truth of this observation.

In Matthew 9, at the second verse, you read of a man that was sick of the palsy; and he was coming to Jesus Christ, being borne upon a bed by his friends. He also was coming himself, and that upon another account than any of his friends were aware of, even for the pardon of sins and the salvation of his soul. Now, as soon as ever he was come into the presence of Christ, Christ tells him, 'Be of good cheer.' It seems then, his heart was fainting; but what was the cause of his fainting? Not his bodily infirmity, for the cure of which his friends did bring him to Christ; but the guilt and burden of his sins, for the pardon of which he himself did come to him; therefore he proceeds, 'Be of good cheer, thy sins be forgiven thee.' I say, Christ saw him sinking in his mind, about how it would go with his most noble part; and therefore, first, he applies himself to him upon that account. For though his friends had faith enough as to the cure of the body, yet he himself had little enough as to the cure of his soul: therefore Christ takes him up as a man falling down, saying, 'Son, be of good cheer, thy sins be forgiven thee.'

That about the Prodigal seems pertinent also to this matter: 'When he came to himself, he said, How many hired servants of my father's have bread enough and to spare, and I perish with hunger! I will arise and go to my father.' Heartily spoken; but how did he perform his promise? Not so well, I think, as he promised to do. And my ground for my thoughts is because his father, as soon as he came to him, fell upon his neck and kissed him. Implying, I think, that the prodigal by this time was dejected in his mind; and therefore his father gives him the most sudden and familiar token of reconciliation. And kisses were in old times often used to remove doubts and fears. Thus Laban and Esau kiss Jacob. Thus Joseph kissed his brethren; and thus also David kissed Absalom (*Gen.* 31:55; 33:1-4; 48:9,10; *2 Sam.* 14:33).

It is true, as I said, that at first setting out, he spoke heartily, as sometimes sinners also do in their beginning to come to Jesus Christ. But might he not have, as in all probability he had, between the first step he took and the last by which he accomplished that journey, many a thought, both this way and that, as to whether his father would receive him or not? As thus: 'I said I would go to my Father. But how if, when I come to him, he should ask me where I have been all this while? What must I say then? Also, if he asks me, 'What is become of the portion of goods that I gave you?' What shall I say then? If he asks me, 'Who have been your companions?' What shall I say then? If he also shall ask me, 'What has your occupation been in all the time of your absence from me?' What shall I say then? Yes, and if he asks me, 'Why did you come home no sooner?', what shall I say then? Thus, I say, might he reason with himself, and being conscious to himself that he could give but a bad answer to any of these interrogatories, no marvel if he stood in need first of all of a kiss from his father's lips. For had he answered these questions truly, he would have to have said, I have been a haunter of taverns and ale-houses; and as for my portion, I spent it in riotous living; my companions were whores and drabs[1]; as for my occupation, the highest was that I became a swine-herd; and as for my not coming home until now, could I have made shift to have stayed abroad any longer, I would not be lying at your feet for mercy now.

I say, these things considered, and on remembering again how prone poor man is to give way, when truly awakened, to despondings and heart misgivings, no marvel if he did sink in his mind, between the time of his first setting out, and that of his coming to his Father.

But, *thirdly*, I think I have for the confirmation of this truth the consent of all the saints that are under heaven, namely, that they that are coming to Jesus Christ, are often heartily afraid that he will not receive them.

QUESTION: But what should be the reason? I will answer this question thus:

1. It is not for want of the revealed will of God that manifests grounds for the contrary, for of that there is a sufficiency. Yes, the text itself has laid a sufficient foundation for encouragement for them that are coming to

[1] Low, sluttish women.

Jesus Christ. 'And him that cometh to me I will in no wise cast out.'

2. It is not for want of any invitation to come, for that is full and plain. 'Come unto me, all ye that labour and are heavy laden, and I will give you rest' (*Matt.* 11:28).

3. Neither is it for want of a manifestation of Christ's willingness to receive, as those texts above named, with that which follows, declare, 'If any man thirst, let him come unto me, and drink' (*John* 7:37).

4. It is not for want of exceeding great and precious promises to receive them that come. 'Therefore come out from among them, and be ye separate, saith the Lord, and touch not the unclean thing, and I will receive you, and will be a Father unto you, and ye shall be my sons and daughters, saith the Lord Almighty' (*2 Cor.* 6:17–18).

5. It is not for want of solemn oath and engagement to save them that come. 'For . . . because he could swear by no greater, he sware by himself . . . that by two immutable things, in which it was impossible for God to lie, we might have a strong consolation, who have fled for refuge to lay hold upon the hope set before us' (*Heb.* 6:13–18).

6. Neither is it for want of great examples of God's mercy, that have come to Jesus Christ, of which we read most plentifully in the Word. Therefore, it must be concluded, it is for want of that which follows.

WHAT IS IT THAT PREVENTS THEM COMING TO CHRIST?

Firstly, it is *want of the knowledge of Christ.*

You know only a little of the grace and kindness that is in the heart of Christ; you know only a little of the virtue and merit of his blood; you know only a little of the willingness that is in his heart to save you; and this is the reason of the fear that arises in your heart, and that causes you to think that Christ will not receive you. Unbelief is the daughter of Ignorance. Therefore Christ says, 'O fools, and slow of heart to believe' (*Luke* 24:25).

Slowness of heart to believe flows from your foolishness in the things of Christ. This is evident to all that are acquainted with themselves, and are seeking after Jesus Christ. The more ignorance, the more unbelief. The more knowledge of Christ, the more faith. 'They that know thy name will put their trust in thee' (*Psa.* 9:10). He, therefore, that began to come to Christ but the other day, and has yet but little knowledge of him, he fears that Christ will not receive him. But he that has been longer acquainted with him, he 'is strong, and has overcome the wicked one' (*1 John* 2:13). When Joseph's brethren came into Egypt to buy corn, it is said, 'Joseph knew his brethren, but his brethren knew not him.' What follows? Why, great mistrust of heart about their prospects, especially, if Joseph answered them roughly, calling them spies and questioning their truth and the like. And observe this, so long as their ignorance about their brother remained with them, whatsoever Joseph did, still they put the worse sense upon it. For instance, Joseph at one time told the steward of his house to bring them home, to dine with him, to dine even in Joseph's house. And how do they take this? Why, they are afraid. 'And the men were afraid, because they were brought unto [their brother] Joseph's house.' And they said, He seeketh occasion against us, and will fall upon us, and take us for bondmen, and our asses (*Gen.* 43:18). What! Afraid to go to Joseph's house? He was their brother; he intended to feast them; to feast them and to feast with them. Ah! But they were ignorant that he was their brother. And so long as their ignorance lasted, so long their fear terrified them.

This is how it is with the sinner that but of late is coming to Jesus Christ. He is ignorant of the love and pity that is in Christ to coming sinners. Therefore he doubts, therefore he fears, therefore his heart misgives him.

Coming sinner, Christ invites you to dine and sup with him. He invites you to a banquet of wine, yes, to come into his wine-cellar, and his banner over you shall be love (*Rev.* 3:20; *Song of Sol.* 2:5). But I doubt it, says the sinner. But, it is answered, he calls you, invites you to his banquet, flagons, apples; to his wine, and to the juice of his pomegranate. 'Oh, I fear, I doubt, I mistrust, I tremble in expectation of the contrary!' Come out of the man, dastardly ignorance! Be not afraid, sinner, only believe; 'He that cometh to Christ, he will in no wise cast out.'

Let the coming sinner, therefore, seek after more of the good knowledge of Jesus Christ. Press after it, seek it as silver, and dig for it as for hidden treasure. This will embolden you; this will make you wax stronger and stronger. 'I know whom I have believed', I know him, said Paul; and what follows? Why, 'And I am persuaded that he is able to keep that which I have committed unto him, against that day' (*2 Tim.* 1:12). What had Paul committed to Jesus Christ? The answer is, he had committed to him his soul. But why did he commit his soul to him? Why, because he knew him. He knew him to be faithful, to be kind. He knew he would not fail him, nor forsake him; and therefore he laid his soul down at his feet, and committed it to him to keep against that day.

Secondly, your fears that Christ will not receive you may be also *a consequent of your earnest and strong desires after your salvation by him.*

For this I observe, that strong desires to have are attended with strong fears of missing. What a man most sets his heart upon, and what his desires are most after, he often most fears he shall not obtain. So the ruler of the synagogue, had a great desire that his daughter should live; and that desire was attended with fear, that she should not. Therefore, Christ says to him, 'Be not afraid' (*Mark* 5:36).

Suppose a young man should have his heart much set upon a maiden to have her as a wife, if ever he fears he shall not obtain her, it is when he begins to love. Now, he thinks, somebody will step in between my love and the object of it; either they will find fault with my person, my estate, or my conditions! Now thoughts begin to work; she does not like me, or something else is wrong. And so it is with the soul at first coming to Jesus Christ. You love him, and your love produces jealousy, and that jealousy often brings forth fears.

Now you fear the sins of your youth, the sins of your old age, the sins of your calling, the sins of your Christian duties, the sins of your heart, or something else. You think something or other will alienate the heart and affections of Jesus Christ from you; you think he sees something in you, for the sake of which he will refuse your soul. But be content, a little more knowledge of him will make you take better heart; your earnest desires shall not be attended with such burning fears; you shall hereafter say, 'This is my infirmity' (*Psa.* 77:10).

You are sick of love, a very sweet disease, and yet every disease has some weakness attending it. But I wish this distemper, if it be lawful to call it so, was more epidemical. Die of this disease I would gladly do; it is better than life itself, though it be attended with fears. But you cry, I cannot obtain. Well, do not be too hasty in making conclusions. If Jesus Christ had not put his finger in at the hole of the lock, your bowels would not have been troubled for him (*Song of Sol.* 5:4). Notice how the prophet has it, 'They shall walk after the LORD; he shall roar like a lion; when he shall roar, then the children shall tremble from the west, they shall tremble as a bird out of Egypt, and as a dove out of the land of Assyria' (*Hos.* 11:10–11). When God roars (as often the coming soul hears him roar), what man that is coming can do otherwise than tremble (*Amos* 3:8)? But trembling he comes: 'He sprang in, and came trembling, and fell down before Paul and Silas' (*Acts* 16:29).

Should you ask the young man that we mentioned just now, How long is it since you began to fear you should miss of this damsel you love so? The answer would be, Ever since I began to love her. But did you not fear it before? No, nor should I fear it now, but that I vehemently love her. Come, sinner, let us apply it: How long is it since you began to fear that Jesus Christ would not receive you? You answer, Ever since I began to desire that he would save my soul. I began to fear, when I began to come; and the more my heart burns in desires after him, the more I feel my heart fear I shall not be saved by him. See now, did I not tell you that your fears were but the consequence of strong desires? Well, fear not, coming sinner, thousands of coming souls are in your condition, and yet they will get safe into Christ's bosom: 'Say', says Christ, 'to them that are of a fearful heart, Be strong, fear not; your God will come and save you' (*Isa.* 35:4; 63:1).

Thirdly, your fear that Christ will not receive you *may arise from a sense of your own unworthiness.*

You see what a poor, sorry, wretched, worthless creature you are; and seeing this, you fear Christ will not receive you. Alas, you say, I am the vilest of all men; a town sinner, a ringleading sinner! I am not only a sinner myself, but have made others twofold worse the children of hell also. Besides, now I am under some awakenings and stirrings of mind after salvation, even now I find my heart rebellious, carnal, hard, treacherous, desperate, prone to unbelief, to despair. It forgets the Word; it wanders; it runs to the ends of the earth. There is not, I am persuaded, one in all the world that has such a desperate wicked heart as mine; my soul is careless to do good, but none more earnest to do that which is evil.

Can such a one as I am, live in glory? Can a holy, a just, and a righteous God, once think (with honour to his Name) of saving such a vile creature as I am? I fear not. Will he show wonders to such a dead dog as I am? I doubt it. I am cast out to the loathing of my person, yes, I loath myself; I stink in my own nostrils. How can I then be accepted by a holy and sin-abhorring God? (*Psa.* 38:5–7; *Ezek.* 11; 20:42,44). Saved I would be; and who is there that would not, were they in my condition? Indeed, I wonder at the madness and folly of others, when I see them leap and skip so carelessly about the mouth of hell! Bold sinner, how dare you tempt God, by laughing at the breach of his holy law?

But alas! they are not so bad in one way, but I am worse in another: I wish myself were anybody but myself; and yet here again, I know not what to wish. When I see such as I believe are coming to Jesus Christ, Oh, I bless them! But I am confounded in myself, to see how unlike, as I think, I am to every good man in the world. They can read, hear, pray, remember, repent, be humble, do everything better than so vile a wretch as I. I, vile wretch, am good for nothing but to burn in hell-fire, and when I think of that, I am confounded too!

Thus the sense of unworthiness creates and heightens fears in the hearts of them that are coming to Jesus Christ. But indeed it should not; for who needs the physician but the sick? Or who did Christ come into the world to save, but the chief of sinners (*Mark* 2:17; *1 Tim*. 1:15)? Therefore, the more you see your sins, the faster you fly to Jesus Christ. And let the sense of your own unworthiness prevail with you to go still faster. As it is with the man that carries his broken arm in a sling to the bone-setter, still as he thinks of his broken arm, and as he feels the pain and anguish, he hastens his pace to the man.

And if Satan meets you, and asks, Where are you going? Tell him you are maimed, and you are going to the Lord Jesus. If he throws at you your own unworthiness, tell him that, even as the sick seek the physician, as he that has broken bones seeks him that can set them, so you are going to Jesus Christ for cure and healing for your sin-sick soul. But it often happens to him that flies for his life, he despairs of escaping, and therefore delivers himself up into the hand of the pursuer. But up, up, sinner; be of good cheer, Christ came to save the unworthy ones: be not faithless, but believe. Come away, man, the Lord Jesus calls you, saying, 'And him that cometh to me I will in no wise cast out.'

Fourthly, your fear that Christ will not receive you, may arise *from a sense of the exceeding mercy of being saved*.

Sometimes salvation is in the eyes of him that desires it so great, so huge, so wonderful a thing, that the very thoughts of the excellency of it engenders unbelief about obtaining it in the heart of those that unfeignedly desire it. 'Seemeth it to you', says David, 'a light thing to be a king's son-in-law?' (*1 Sam.* 18:23). So the thoughts of the greatness and glory of the thing offered, as heaven, eternal life, eternal glory, to be with God, and Christ, and angels; these are great things, things too good, says the soul that is little in his own eyes. Things too rich for me, says the soul that is truly poor in spirit.

Besides, the Holy Ghost has a way of enlarging heavenly things to the understanding of the coming sinner; yes, and at the same time of enlarging too, the sin and unworthiness of that sinner. Now the soul staggeringly wonders, saying, What! To be made like angels, like Christ, to live in eternal bliss, joy, and felicity! This is for angels, and for them that can walk like angels! If a prince, a duke, an earl, should send (by the hand of his servant) for some poor, sorry, beggarly drudge, to take her as a wife for his master, and the servant should come and say, My lord and master has sent me to you, to take you to him to wife; he is rich, beautiful, and of excellent qualities; he is loving, meek, humble, well-spoken, etc. What now would this poor, sorry, beggarly creature think? What would she say? Or how would she frame an answer?

When king David sent to Abigail upon this account, and though she was a rich woman, yet she said, 'Behold, let thine handmaid be a servant to wash the feet of the servants of my lord' (*1 Sam.* 25:40,41). She was confounded, she did not know what to say, the offer was so great, beyond what could in reason be expected.

But suppose this great person should second his suit, and send to this sorry creature again, what would she say now? Would she not say, 'You mock me'? But what if he affirms that he is in earnest, and that his lord must have her to wife. Yes, suppose he should prevail upon her to believe his message, and to address herself for her journey; yet, behold every thought of her pedigree confounds her. Also her sense of want of beauty makes her ashamed; and if she just thinks of being embraced, the unbelief that is mixed with that thought whirls her into tremblings. And now she calls herself a fool, for believing the messenger, and thinks of not going. If she thinks of being bold, she blushes; and the least thought that she shall be rejected, when she comes to him, makes her look as if she would give up the ghost.

And is it a wonder then, to see a soul that is drowned in the sense of glory and a sense of its own nothingness, to be confounded in itself, and to fear that the glory apprehended is too great, too good, and too rich, for such a one? That thing, heaven and eternal glory, is so great, and I that would have it, so small, so sorry a creature, that the thoughts of obtaining it confounds me.

Thus, I say, does the greatness of the things desired, quite dash and overthrow the mind of the desirer. Oh, it is too big! It is too big! It is too great a mercy! But, coming sinner, let me reason with you. You say, it is too big, too great. Well, will things that are less satisfy your soul? Will a less thing than heaven, than glory and eternal life, answer your desires? No, nothing less. And yet I fear they are too big, and too good for me, ever to obtain. Well, as big and as good as they are, God gives them to such as you; they are not too big for God to give; no, not too big to give freely. Be content; let God give like himself; he is that eternal God, and gives like himself.

When kings give, they do not give in the way that poor men do. Hence it is said, that Nabal made a feast in his house like the feast of a king; and again, 'All these things did Araunah, as a king, give unto David' (*2 Sam.* 25:36; *2 Sam.* 24:23). Now, God is a great king, let him give like a king; no, let him give like himself, and may you receive like yourself. He has all, and you have nothing. God told his people of old that he would save them in truth and in righteousness, and that they should return to, and enjoy the land, which before, for their sins, had spewed them out. And then he adds, under a sense of their counting the mercy too good, or too big, 'If it be marvellous in the eyes of the remnant of this people in these days, should it also be marvellous in mine eyes? saith the LORD of hosts' (*Zech.* 8:6).

It is as if someone should say, they are now in captivity, and little in their own eyes; therefore they think the mercy of returning to Canaan is a mercy too marvellously big for them to enjoy. 'But if it be so in their eyes,' saith God, 'it is not so in mine; I will do for them like God, if they will but receive my bounty like sinners.' Coming sinner, God can give his heavenly Canaan, and the glory of it, to you; yes, none ever had them but as a gift, a free gift. He has given us his Son, 'How shall he not with him also freely give us all things?' (*Rom.* 8:32).

It was not the worthiness of Abraham, or Moses, or David or Peter, or Paul, but the mercy of God, that made them inheritors of heaven. If God thinks you worthy, judge not yourself unworthy; but take it, and be thankful. And it is a good sign he intends to give you, if he has drawn out your heart to ask. 'LORD, thou hast heard the desire of the humble; thou wilt prepare their heart; thou wilt cause thine ear to hear' (*Psa.* 10:17).

When God is said to incline his ear, it implies an intention to bestow the mercy desired. Take it therefore; your wisdom will be to receive, not sticking at your own unworthiness. It is said, 'He raiseth up the poor out of the dust, and lifteth up the beggar from the dunghill, to set them among princes, and to make them inherit the throne of glory.' Again, 'He raiseth up the poor out of the dust, and lifteth the needy out of the dunghill, that he may set him with princes, even with the princes of his people' (*1 Sam.* 2:8; *Psa.* 113:7,8). You see also when God made a wedding for his Son, he called not the great, nor the rich, nor the mighty; but the poor, the maimed, the halt, and the blind (*Matt.* 12; *Luke* 14).

Fifthly, your fears that Christ will not receive you *may arise from the hideous roaring of the devil,* who pursues you. He that hears him roar, must be a mighty Christian, if he can at that time deliver himself from fear. He is called a roaring lion; and then, to allude to that in Isaiah, 'They shall roar against them like the roaring of the sea; and if one look [into them, they have] darkness and sorrow, and the light is darkened in the heavens thereof' (*1 Pet.* 5:8; *Isa.* 5:30).

There are two things among many that Satan uses to roar out after them that are coming to Jesus Christ.

1. *That they are not elected.* Or, 2. *That they have sinned the sin against the Holy Ghost.* To both these I answer briefly:

1. *On the subject of election*, out of which you fear you are excluded, why, coming sinner, even the text itself affords you help against this doubt, and that by a double argument.

i. That coming to Christ is by virtue of the gift, promise, and drawing of the Father; but you are coming; therefore God has given you, promised you, and is drawing you to Jesus Christ. Coming sinner, hold to this; and when Satan begins to roar again, answer, But I feel my heart moving after Jesus Christ; but that would not be, if it were not given by promise, and drawing to Christ by the power of the Father.

ii. Jesus Christ has promised that 'him that cometh to him he will in no wise cast out'. And if he has said it, will he not make it good, I mean even your salvation? For, as I have said already, not to cast out, is to receive and admit to the benefit of salvation. If then the Father has given you, as is manifest by your coming; and if Christ will receive you, coming soul, as it is plain he will, because he has said, 'I will in no wise cast out'; then be confident and let those conclusions that as naturally flow from the text as light from the sun, or water from the fountain, support you.

If Satan therefore objects, But you are not elected, answer, But I am coming, Satan, I am coming; and that I could not be, but that the Father draws me; and I am coming to such a Lord Jesus, as will in no wise cast me out. Further, Satan, if I were not elect, the Father would not draw me, nor would the Son so graciously open his bosom to me. I am persuaded, that not one of the non-elect shall ever be able to say, no, not in the day of judgment, I did sincerely come to Jesus Christ. Come they may, feignedly, as Judas and Simon Magus did; but that is not our question. Therefore, O honest-hearted coming sinner, be not afraid, but come.

2. *On the subject of the sin against the Holy Ghost*: As to the second part of the objection, about sinning the sin against the Holy Ghost, the same argument overthrows that also.

i. Coming to Christ is by virtue of a special gift of the Father; but the Father gives no such gift to them that have sinned that sin; therefore you who are coming have not committed that sin. That the Father gives no such gift to them that have sinned that sin is evident:

a. Because such have sinned themselves out of God's favour. They shall never have forgiveness (*Matt.* 12:32). But it is a special favour of God to give to a man, to come to Jesus Christ, because by so doing he obtains forgiveness. Therefore he that comes has not sinned that sin.

b. Because they that have sinned the sin against the Holy Ghost have sinned themselves out of an interest in the sacrifice of Christ's body and blood; 'There remaineth no more sacrifice for sins' (*Heb.* 10:26). But God does not give grace to any of them to come to Christ that have no share in the sacrifice of his body and blood. Therefore, you who are coming to him, have not sinned that sin.

ii. Coming to Christ is by the special drawing of the Father; 'No man can come to me except the Father which has sent me draw him' (*John* 6:44). But the Father draws not him to Christ for whom he has not allotted forgiveness by his blood; therefore they that are coming to Jesus Christ have not committed that sin, because he has allotted them forgiveness by his blood. That the Father cannot draw them to Jesus Christ for whom he has not allotted forgiveness of sins is manifest to sense; for that would be a plain mockery, a fable, neither becoming his wisdom, justice, holiness, nor goodness.

iii. Coming to Jesus Christ lays a man under the promise of forgiveness and salvation. But it is impossible that he that has sinned that sin should ever be put under a promise of these. Therefore, he that has sinned that sin can never have a heart to come to Jesus Christ.

iv. Coming to Jesus Christ lays a man under his intercession. 'For he ever liveth to make intercession for them that come' (*Heb.* 7:25). Therefore, he that is coming to Jesus Christ cannot have sinned that sin. Christ has forbidden his people to pray for them that have sinned that sin; and, therefore, will not pray for them himself, but he prays for them that come.

v. He that has sinned that sin, Christ is to him of no more worth than is a man that is dead, for he has crucified to himself the Son of God, and has also counted his precious blood as the blood of an unholy thing (see Hebrews 6 and 10). Now, he that has this low esteem of Christ will never come to him for life; but the coming man has a high esteem of his Person, blood, and merits. Therefore, he that is coming has not committed that sin.

vi. If he that has sinned this sin might yet come to Jesus Christ, then must the truth of God be overthrown which says in one place, 'He has never forgiveness', and in another, 'I will in no wise cast him out.' Therefore, that he may never have forgiveness, he shall never have heart to come to Jesus Christ. It is impossible that such a one should be renewed, either to or by repentance (*Heb.* 6). Therefore, never trouble your head nor heart about this matter; he that comes to Jesus Christ cannot have sinned against the Holy Ghost.

Sixthly, your fears that Christ will not receive you *may arise from your own folly*, in inventing, yes, in your chalking out to God, a way to bring you home to Jesus Christ. Some souls that are coming to Jesus Christ are great tormentors of themselves upon this account; they conclude that, if their coming to Jesus Christ is right, they have to be brought home in such and such a way.

For instance, says one:

If God is bringing me to Jesus Christ, then will he load me with the guilt of sin till he makes me roar again.

If God is indeed a bringing me home to Jesus Christ, then I must be assaulted with dreadful temptations of the devil.

If God is indeed a-bringing me to Jesus Christ, then, even as I am coming to him, I shall have wonderful revelations of him.

This is the way that some sinners appoint for God; but perhaps he will not walk in that way; yet will he bring them to Jesus Christ. But now, because they come not the way of their own chalking out, they are at a loss. They look for heavy load and burden; but, perhaps, God gives them a sight of their lost condition, and adds not that heavy weight and burden. They look for fearful temptations of Satan; but God sees that yet they are not fit for them, nor is the time come that he should be honoured by them in such a condition. They look for great and glorious revelations of Christ, grace, and mercy; but, perhaps, God only takes the yoke from off their jaws, and lays meat before them. And now again they are at a loss, yet a coming to Jesus Christ. 'I drew them', says God, 'with cords of a man, with bands of love: and I was to them as they that take off the yoke on their jaws, and I laid meat unto them' (*Hos.* 11:4).

Now, I say, If God brings you to Christ, and not by the way that you have appointed, then you are at a loss; and for your being at a loss you may thank yourself. God has more ways than you know of to bring a sinner to Jesus Christ; but he will not give you beforehand an account by which of them he will bring you to Christ (*Isa.* 40:13; *Job* 33:13). Sometimes he has his ways in the whirlwind; but sometimes the Lord is not there (*Nah.* 1:3; *1 Kings* 19:11). If God will deal more gently with you than with others of his children, grudge not at it; refuse not the waters that go softly, lest he bring upon you the waters of the rivers, strong and many, even these two smoking firebrands, the devil and guilt of sin (*Isa.* 8:6–7). He says to Peter, 'Follow me.' And what thunder did Zacchæus hear or see? 'Zacchæus, Come down,' said Christ. 'And he came down,' says Luke, 'and received him joyfully.'

But had Peter or Zacchæus made the objection that you have made, and directed the Spirit of the Lord as you have done, they might have looked long enough before they had found themselves coming to Jesus Christ.

Besides, I will tell you, that the greatness of sense of sin, the hideous roaring of the devil, yes, and abundance of revelations, will not prove that God is bringing your soul to Jesus Christ; as Balaam, Cain, Judas, and others, can witness.

Further, consider that what you have not of these things here, you may have another time, and that to your distraction. Therefore, instead of being discontent, because you are not in the fire, because you hear not the sound of the trumpet and alarm of war: 'Pray that ye enter not into temptation.' Yes, come boldly to the throne of grace, and obtain mercy, and find grace to help in that time of need (*Psa.* 88:15; *Matt.* 26:41; *Heb.* 4:16).

Poor creature! You cry, 'If I were tempted, I could come faster and with more confidence to Christ.' You do not know what you are saying. What says Job? 'Withdraw thine hand far from me: and let not thy dread make me afraid. Then call thou, and I will answer: or let me speak, and answer thou me' (*Job* 13:21–22). It is not the over-heavy load of sin, but the discovery of mercy; not the roaring of the devil, but the drawing of the Father, that makes a man come to Jesus Christ. I myself know all these things.

True, sometimes, yes, regularly, they that come to Jesus Christ come the way that you desire; the loading, tempted way; but the Lord also leads some by the waters of comfort. If I was to choose when to go on a long journey, namely, whether I would go in the dead of winter or in the pleasant spring (though, if it was a very profitable journey, as that of coming to Christ is, I would choose to go it through fire and water before I would choose to lose the benefit.) But, I say, if I might choose the time, I would choose to go in the pleasant spring, because the way would be more delightful, the days longer and warmer, the nights shorter and not so cold. And it is observable that that very argument that you use to weaken your strength in the way, that very argument Christ Jesus uses to encourage his beloved to come to him: 'Rise up,' says he, 'my love, my fair one, and come away.' Why? 'For lo, the winter is past, the rain is over and gone; the flowers appear on the earth, the time of the singing of birds is come, and the voice of the turtle is heard in our land; the fig-tree putteth forth her green figs, and the vines with the tender grape give a good smell. Arise, my love, my fair one, and come away' (*Song of Sol.* 2:10–13).

Trouble not yourself, coming sinner. If you see your lost condition by original and actual sin; if you see your need of the spotless righteousness of Jesus Christ; if you are willing to be found in him, and to take up your cross and follow him; then pray for a fair wind and good weather, and come away. Stick no longer in a muse and doubt about things, but come away to Jesus Christ. Do it, I say, lest you tempt God to lay the sorrows of a travailing woman upon you. Your folly in this thing may make him do it. Mind what follows: 'The sorrows of a travailing woman shall come upon him.' Why? 'He is an unwise son; for he should not stay long in the place of the breaking forth of children' (*Hos.* 13:13).

Seventhly, your fears that Christ will not receive you *may arise from those decays that you find in your soul,* even while you are coming to him. You fear that you do not run fast enough. Some, even as they are coming to Jesus Christ, find themselves growing worse and worse; and this is indeed a sore trial to the poor coming sinner.

To explain myself. There could be a man coming to Jesus Christ who, when at first he began to look out for him, was sensible, affectionate, and broken in spirit; but now is grown dark, senseless, hard-hearted, and inclining to neglect spiritual duties, etc. Furthermore, he now finds inclinations in himself to unbelief, atheism, blasphemy and the like. He finds now that he cannot tremble at God's Word and his judgment, nor at the apprehension of hell fire; neither can he, as he thinks, be sorry for these things. Now, this is a sad dispensation.

The man under the sixth head complains for want of temptations, but this man has enough of them. Are you glad of them, tempted, coming sinner? Those that were never exercised with them may think it a fine thing to be within the range, but he that is there is ready to sweat blood for sorrow of heart, and to howl for vexation of spirit! This man is in the wilderness among wild beasts. Here he sees a bear, there a lion, yonder a leopard, a wolf, a dragon; devils of all sorts, doubts of all sorts, fears of all sorts, haunt and molest his soul. Here he sees smoke, yes, feels fire and brimstone, scattered upon his secret places. He hears the sound of a horrible tempest. Oh, my friends, even the Lord Jesus, that knew all things, even he saw no pleasure in temptations, nor did he desire to be with them; therefore, one text says, 'He was led', and another, 'He was driven', of the Spirit into the wilderness, to be tempted of the devil (*Matt.* 4:1; *Mark* 1:12).

But to return. Thus it happens sometimes to them that are coming to Jesus Christ. A sad hap indeed! One would think that he that is flying from wrath to come has little need of such clogs as these. And yet so it is, and woeful experience proves it. The church of old complained that her enemies overtook her between the straits; just between hope and fear, heaven and hell (*Lam.* 1).

This man feels the infirmity of his flesh, he finds a proneness in himself to be desperate. Now he chides with God, flings and tumbles like a wild bull in a net, and still the guilt of all returns upon himself, to the crushing of him to pieces. Yet he feels his heart so hard, that he can find, as he thinks, no kind falling under any of his miscarriages. Now he is a lump of confusion in his own eyes, whose spirit and actions are without order.

Temptations serve the Christian as the shepherd's dog serves the silly sheep; that is, coming behind the flock, he runs upon it, pulls it down, worries it, wounds it, and grievously bedabbles it with dirt and wet, in the lowest places of the furrows of the field, not leaving it until it is half dead, nor then either, except for God's rebuke.

Here is now room for fears of being cast away. Now I see I am lost, says the sinner. This is not coming to Jesus Christ, says the sinner; such a desperate, hard, and wretched heart as mine is, cannot be a gracious one, says the sinner. And to command such a heart to be better, he says, I cannot; no, I cannot.

QUESTION: But what will you say to a soul in this condition?

ANSWER: I will say that temptations have attended the

best of God's people, that temptations come to do us good, and that there is a difference between growing worse and worse and your seeing more clearly how bad you are.

Consider a man with an ugly appearance who has too high a conceit of his beauty; and, without the benefit of a mirror, he still stands in his own conceit. At last an artist is sent to him, who draws his ill-favoured face to the life; now looking at it, he begins to be convinced that he is not half so handsome as he thought he was. Coming sinner, your temptations are these painters; they have drawn out your ill-favoured heart to the life, and have set it before your eyes, and now you see how ill-favoured you are. Hezekiah was a good man, yet when he lay sick, for all that I know, he had too good an opinion of his heart. And for all I know also, the Lord might, upon his recovery, leave him to a temptation, that he might better know all that was in his heart. Compare Isaiah 38:1-3 with 2 Chronicles 32:31.

Alas! We are sinful out of measure, but see it not to the full until an hour of temptation comes. But when it comes, it does as the painter does, draws out our heart to the life. Yet the sight of what we are should not keep us from coming to Jesus Christ. There are two ways by which God lets a man into a sight of the wickedness of his heart; one is *by the light of the Word and Spirit of God*; and the other is *by the temptations of the devil*. But by the first, we see our wickedness one way; and, by the second, another way. By the light of the Word and Spirit of God, you have a sight of your wickedness; and by the light of the sun, you have a sight of the spots and defilements that are in your house or raiment. This light enables you to see a need of cleansing, but does not make the blemishes spread more abominably. But when Satan comes, when he tempts, he puts life and rage into our sins, and turns them, as it were, into so many devils within us. Now, like prisoners, they attempt to break through the prison of our body; they will attempt to get out at our eyes, mouth, ears, by any way, to the scandal of the gospel, and reproach of religion, to the darkening of our evidences, and damning of our souls.

But I shall say, as I said before, this has often been the lot of God's people. And, 'There hath no temptation taken you but such as is common to man: but God is faithful, who will not suffer you to be tempted above that ye are able' (*1 Cor.* 10:13). See the Book of Job, the Book of Psalms, and that of the Lamentations. And remember further, that Christ himself was tempted to blaspheme, to worship the devil, and to murder himself (*Matt.* 4; *Luke* 4); temptations worse than which you can hardly be overtaken with. But he was sinless, that is true. And he is your Saviour, and that is as true! Yes, it is as true also that, by his being tempted, he became the conqueror of the tempter, and a succourer of those that are tempted (*Col.* 2:14,15; *Heb.* 2:15; 4:15–16).

QUESTION: But what should be the reason that some that are coming to Christ should be so lamentably cast down and buffeted with temptations?

ANSWER: It may be for several causes.

1. Some that are coming to Christ cannot be persuaded, until the temptation comes, that they are so vile as the Scripture says they are. True, they see so much of their wretchedness as to drive them to Christ. But there is an over and above of wickedness which they see not. Peter little thought that he had cursing, and swearing, and lying, and an inclination in his heart to deny his Master, before the temptation came; but when that indeed came upon him, then he found it there to his sorrow (*John* 13:36–38; *Mark* 14:36–40, 68–72).

2. Some that are coming to Jesus Christ are too much affected with their own graces, and too little taken with Christ's Person. Therefore God, to take them off from doting upon their own jewels, and that they might look more to the Person, undertaking, and merits of his Son, plunges them into the ditch by temptations. And this I take to be the meaning of Job, 'If I wash myself', said he, 'with snow water, and make my hands never so clean, yet shalt thou plunge me in the ditch, and mine own clothes shall abhor me' (*Job* 9:30–31). Job had been a little too much tampering with his own graces, and setting his excellencies a little too high, as these texts make manifest: *Job* 33:8–13; 34:5–10; 35:2–3; 38:1–2; 40:1–5, 42:3–6. But by the time the temptations were ended, you find him better taught.

Yes, God often, even for this thing, takes as it were our graces from us, and so leaves us almost completely to ourselves and to the tempter, that we may learn not to love the picture more than the Person of his Son. See how he dealt with them in Ezekiel 16 and in Hosea 2.

3. Perhaps you have been given too much to judging your brother, to condemning your brother, because he is a poor tempted man. And God, to bring down the pride of your heart, lets the tempter loose upon you, that you also may feel yourself weak. For 'pride goeth before destruction, and an haughty spirit before a fall' (*Prov.* 16:18).

4. It may be you have dealt a little too roughly with those that God has this way wounded, not considering yourself, lest you also be tempted. And therefore God has suffered it to come to you (*Gal.* 6:1).

5. It may be you were given to slumber and sleep, and therefore these temptations were sent to awaken you. You know that Peter's temptation came upon him after his sleeping; then, instead of watching and praying, then he denied, and denied, and denied his Master (*Matt.* 26).

6. It may be you have presumed too much, and stood too much in your own strength, and therefore a time of temptation has come upon you. This was also one cause why it came upon Peter – 'Though all men forsake thee, yet will not I.' Ah! That is the way to be tempted indeed (*John* 13:36–38).

7. It may be God intends to make you wise, to speak a word in season to others that are afflicted; and therefore

he suffers you to be tempted. Christ was tempted that he might be able to succour them that are tempted (*Heb.* 2:18).

8. It may be Satan has dared God to suffer him to tempt you; promising himself that if God will but let him do it, you will curse God to his face. Thus he obtained leave against Job; therefore take heed, tempted soul, lest you prove the devil's sayings true (*Job* 1:11).

9. It may be that your graces must be tried in the fire, so that the rust that cleaves to them may be taken away, and themselves proved, both before angels and devils, to be far better than gold that perishes. It may be also, that your graces are to receive special praises, and honour, and glory, at the coming of the Lord Jesus to judgment, for all the exploits that you have acted by them against hell and its infernal crew, in the day of your temptation (*1 Pet.* 1:6–7).

10. It may be God would have others learn by your sighs, groans, and complaints, under temptation, to beware of those sins for the sake of which you are at present delivered to the tormentors.

But to conclude this, put the worst to the worst – and then things will be bad enough – suppose that you are to this day without the grace of God, yet you are but a miserable creature, a sinner, that has need of a blessed Saviour. And the text presents you with one as good and kind as the heart could wish; who also for your encouragement says, 'And him that cometh to me I will in no wise cast out.'

THE APPLICATION OF OBSERVATION 2

To come, therefore, to a word of application. Is it so, that they that are coming to Jesus Christ are often heartily afraid that Jesus Christ will not receive them? Then this teacheth us these things:

1. That faith and doubting may at the same time have their residence in the same soul. 'O thou of little faith, wherefore didst thou doubt?' (*Matt.* 14:31). He says not, O thou of no faith! But, O thou of little faith! Because he had a little faith in the midst of his many doubts. The same is true even of many that are coming to Jesus Christ. They come, and fear that they come not, and doubt that they come not. When they look upon the promise, or a word of encouragement by faith, then they come; but when they look upon themselves, or the difficulties that lie before them, then they doubt.

'Bid me come', said Peter; 'Come', said Christ. So he went down out of the ship to go to Jesus, but his fate was to go to him upon the water; there was the trial. So it is with the poor desiring soul. Tell me to come, says the sinner; Come, says Christ, and I will in no wise cast you out. So he comes, but his fate is to come upon the water, upon drowning difficulties; if, therefore, the wind of temptations blow, the waves of doubts and fears will presently arise, and this coming sinner will begin to sink, if he has but little faith. But you shall find here in Peter's little faith, a twofold act; namely, coming and crying. Little faith cannot come all the way without crying. So long as its holy boldness lasts, so long it can come with peace; but when it is so, it can come no further, it will go the rest of the way by crying. Peter went as far as his little faith would carry him: he also cried as far as his little faith would help, 'Lord, save me, I perish!' And so with coming and crying he was kept from sinking, though he had but a little faith. 'Jesus stretched forth his hand, and caught him, and said unto him, O thou of little faith, wherefore didst thou doubt?'

2. Is it so, that they that are coming to Jesus Christ are often heartily afraid that Jesus Christ will not receive them?

Then this shows us a reason of that dejection, and those castings down that, very often, we perceive to be in them that are coming to Jesus Christ. Why, it is because they are afraid that Jesus Christ will not receive them. The poor world, they mock us, because we are a dejected people; I mean, because we are sometimes so. But they do not know the cause of our dejection. Could we be persuaded, even then, when we are dejected, that Jesus Christ would indeed receive us, it would make us fly over their heads, and would put more gladness into our hearts than in the time in which their corn, wine, and oil increases (*Psa.* 4:6–7).

3. Is it so, that they that are coming to Jesus Christ are often heartily afraid that he will not receive them. Then this shows that they that are coming to Jesus Christ are an awakened, sensible, considering people. For fear comes from sense, and from a consideration of things. They are sensible of sin, sensible of the curse due to it; they are also sensible of the glorious majesty of God, and of what a blessed, blessed thing it is to be received of Jesus Christ. The glory of heaven, and the evil of sin, these things they consider, and are sensible of. 'When I remember, I am afraid.' 'When I consider, I am afraid' (*Job* 21:6; 23:15).

These things dash their spirits, being awake and sensible. Were they dead, like other men, they would not be afflicted with fear as they are. For dead men fear not, feel not, care not, but the living and sensible man, he it is that is often heartily afraid that Jesus Christ will not receive him. I say, the dead and senseless are not distressed. They presume; they are groundlessly confident. Who so bold as blind Bayard?[1] These indeed should fear and be afraid, because they are not coming to Jesus Christ. Oh! the hell, the fire, the pit, the wrath of God, and torment of hell, that are prepared for poor neglecting sinners! 'How shall we escape if we neglect so great salvation?' (*Heb.* 2:3). But they lack the sense of things, and so cannot fear.

4. Is it so, that they that are coming to Jesus Christ are often heartily afraid that he will not receive them? Then

---

[1] Pierre du Terrail, Chevalier de Bayard (1473–1534), a French soldier of great courage.

this should teach old Christians to pity and pray for young comers. You know the heart of a stranger; for you yourselves were strangers in the land of Egypt. You know the fears, and doubts, and terrors that take hold of them; in that they at times took hold of you.

Therefore pity them, pray for them, encourage them; they need all this: guilt has overtaken them, fears of the wrath of God have overtaken them. Perhaps they are within the sight of hell fire; and the fear of going there is burning hot within their hearts. You may know, how strangely Satan is suggesting his devilish doubts to them, that if possible he may sink and drown them with the multitude and weight of them. Old Christians, mend up the path for them, take the stumblingblocks out of the way; lest that which is feeble and weak be turned aside, but let it rather be healed (*Heb.* 12).

I come now to the next observation, and shall speak a little to that, namely, *that Jesus Christ would not have them that in truth are coming to him once think that he will cast them out.*

The text is full of this: for he says, 'And him that cometh to me I will in no wise cast out.' Now, if he says, I will not, he would not have us think he will. This is yet further manifest by these considerations.

1. Christ Jesus did forbid even them that as yet were not coming to him, once to think him such an one. 'Do not think,' said he, 'that I will accuse you to the Father' (*John* 5:45).

These, as I said, were such that, as yet, were not coming to him. For he says of them a little before, 'And ye will not come to me'; for the respect they had to the honour of men kept them back. Yet, I say, Jesus Christ gives them to understand that, though he might justly reject them, yet he would not, but bids them not to think once that he would accuse them to the Father. Now, not to accuse, with Christ, is to plead for. For Christ in these things does not stand neutrally between the Father and sinners. So then, if Jesus Christ would not have those that yet will not come to him think that he will accuse them, then he would not have those think so that in truth are coming to him. 'And him that cometh to me I will in no wise cast out.'

2. When the woman taken in adultery, even in the very act, was brought before Jesus Christ, he so behaved both by words and actions that he evidently enough made it manifest that he came not into the world in order to condemn and cast out. Therefore, when they had set her before him, and had accused her of this heinous act, he stooped down, and with his finger wrote upon the ground, as though he heard them not. Now what did he do by this behaviour, but testify plainly that he was not for receiving accusations against poor sinners, whoever were the accusers?

And observe, though they continue asking, thinking at last to force him to condemn her; yet then he so answered that he drove all condemning persons from her. And then he adds, for her encouragement to come to him:

'Neither do I condemn thee; go, and sin no more' (*John* 8:1–11). Not but that he indeed abhorred the deed, but he would not condemn the woman for the sin, because that was not his office. He was not sent 'into the world to condemn the world; but that the world through him might be saved' (*John* 3:17). Now if Christ, though urged to it, would not condemn the guilty woman, though she was far at present from coming to him, he would not that they should once think that he will cast them out that in truth are coming to him. 'And him that cometh to me I will in no wise cast out.'

3. Christ plainly bids the turning sinner come; and forbids him to entertain any such thought as that he will cast him out. 'Let the wicked forsake his way, and the unrighteous man his thoughts; and let him return unto the LORD, and he will have mercy upon him; and to our God, for he will abundantly pardon' (*Isa.* 55:7). The Lord, by bidding the unrighteous forsake his thoughts, particularly forbids, as I have said, those thoughts that hinder the coming man in his progress to Jesus Christ, his unbelieving thoughts. Therefore he bids him not only forsake his ways, but his thoughts. 'Let the wicked forsake his way, and the unrighteous man his thoughts.'

It is not enough to forsake one if you would come to Jesus Christ; because the other will keep you from him. Suppose a man forsakes his wicked ways, his debauched and filthy life; yet if these thoughts, that Jesus Christ will not receive him, be entertained and nourished in his heart, these thoughts will keep him from coming to Jesus Christ.

Sinner, coming sinner, are you for coming to Jesus Christ? Yes, says the sinner. Forsake your wicked ways then. So I do, says the sinner. Why then do you come so slowly? Because I am hindered. What hinders? Has God forbidden you? No. Are you not willing to come faster? Yes, yet I cannot. Well, I pray you, be plain with me, and tell me the reason and ground of your discouragement. Why, says the sinner, though God forbids me not, and though I am willing to come faster, yet there naturally arises this, that and the other thought in my heart, that hinders my speed to Jesus Christ. Sometimes I think I am not chosen; sometimes I think I am not called; sometimes I think I am come too late; and sometimes I think I know not what it is to come. Also the thought that I have no grace; and then again, that I cannot pray; and then again, that I am a real hypocrite. And these things keep me from coming to Jesus Christ.

Look now, did not I tell you so? There are thoughts yet remaining in the heart, even of those who have forsaken their wicked ways; and with those thoughts they are more plagued than with anything else, because they hinder their coming to Jesus Christ. For the sin of unbelief, which is the original of all these thoughts, is that which besets a coming sinner more easily, than does his ways (*Heb.* 12:1–4). But now, since Jesus Christ commands you to forsake these thoughts, forsake them, coming sinner; and if you forsake them not, you transgress the commands of Christ, and remain your own tormentor, and keep yourself from establishment in grace. 'If ye will not believe, surely ye shall not be established' (*Isa.* 7:9). Thus you see how Jesus Christ sets himself against such thoughts as in any way discourage the coming sinner. And this truly vindicates the doctrine we have in hand, namely, that Jesus Christ would not have them that in truth are coming to him once think that he will cast them out. 'And him that cometh to me I will in no wise cast out.'

REASONS FOR OBSERVATION 3

I come now to the reasons of the observation.

1. If Jesus Christ should allow you once to think that he will cast you out, he must allow you to think that he will falsify his Word; for he has said, 'I will in no wise cast out.' But Christ would not that you should count him as one that will falsify his Word; for he says of himself, 'I am the truth;' therefore he would not that any that in truth are coming to him, should once think that he will cast them out.

2. If Jesus Christ should allow the sinner that in truth is coming to him once to think that he will cast him out, then he must allow, and so countenance, the first appearance of unbelief, which he counts his greatest enemy and against which he has employed even his holy gospel. Therefore Jesus Christ would not that they that in truth are coming to him should once think that he will cast them out. See Matthew 14:31; 21:21; Mark 11:23; Luke 24:25.

3. If Jesus Christ should allow the coming sinner once to think that he will cast him out; then he must allow him to question whether he is willing to receive his Father's gift. For the coming sinner is his Father's gift; as also says the text; but he testifies, 'All that the Father giveth me shall come to me; and him that cometh to me I will in no wise cast out.' Therefore Jesus Christ would not have him that in truth is coming to him once to think that he will cast him out.

4. If Jesus Christ should allow them once to think, that indeed are coming to him, that he will cast them out, he must allow them to think that he will despise and reject the drawing of his Father. For no man can come to him but whom the Father draws. But it would be high blasphemy, and damnable wickedness once to imagine this. Therefore, Jesus Christ would not have him that comes once think that he will cast him out.

5. If Jesus Christ should allow those that indeed are coming to him, once to think that he will cast them out, he must allow them to think that he will be unfaithful to the trust and charge that his Father has committed to him; which is to save, and not to lose anything of that which he has given to him to save (*John* 6:39).

But the Father has given him a charge to save the coming sinner; therefore it cannot be that he should allow that such a one should once think that he will cast him out.

6. If Jesus Christ should allow that they should once think, that are coming to him, that he will cast them out, then he must allow them to think that he will be unfaithful to his office of priesthood; for as, by the first part of it, he paid the price for, and ransomed souls, so, by the second part of it, he continually makes intercession to God for them that come (*Heb.* 7:25). But he cannot allow us to question his faithful execution of his priesthood. Therefore he cannot allow us once to think that the coming sinner shall be cast out.

7. If Jesus Christ should allow us once to think that the coming sinner shall be cast out, then he must allow us to question his will, or power, or merit to save. But he cannot allow us once to question any of these; therefore not once to think that the coming sinner shall be cast out.

He cannot allow them to question *his will*; for he says in the text, 'I WILL in no wise cast out.'

He cannot allow us to question *his power*; for the Holy Ghost says HE IS ABLE to save to the uttermost them that come.

He cannot allow them to question *the efficacy of his merit*; for the blood of Christ cleanseth the comer from all sin (*1 John* 1:7), therefore he cannot allow that he that is coming to him should once think that he will cast them out.

8. If Jesus Christ should allow the coming sinner once to think that he will cast him out, he must allow him to

give the lie to the manifest testimony of the Father, the Son, and the Spirit. Yes, to the whole gospel contained in Moses, the prophets, the book of Psalms, and that commonly called the New Testament. But he cannot allow this; therefore, neither that the coming sinner should once think that he will cast him out.

9. Lastly, if Jesus Christ should allow him that is coming to him once to think that he will cast him out, he must allow him to question his Father's oath, which he in truth and righteousness has taken, that they might have a strong consolation who have fled for refuge to Jesus Christ. But he cannot allow this; therefore he cannot allow that the coming sinner should once think that he will cast him out (*Heb.* 6:16–20).

8

The Doctrine
Applied

*'All that the Father giveth me shall come to me; and him
that cometh to me I will in no wise cast out'*
(John 6:37).

I come now to make some general use and application
of the whole, and so to draw towards a conclusion.

THE FIRST USE: INFORMATION

First, the text informs us that *men by nature are far from
Christ.* Let me a little improve this use, by speaking to
these three questions. 1. *Where is he that is coming, but
has not come, to Jesus Christ?* 2. *What is he that is not
coming to Jesus Christ?* 3. *Where is he to go that comes
not to Jesus Christ?*

1. *Where is he?*

He is far from God, he is without him, even alienated from him both in his understanding, will, affections, judgment, and conscience (*Eph.* 2:12; 4:18).

He is far from Jesus Christ, who is the only deliverer of men from hell fire (*Psa.* 73:27).

He is far from the work of the Holy Ghost, the work of regeneration, and a second creation, without which no man shall see the kingdom of heaven (*John* 3:3).

He is far from righteousness, namely, that righteousness that should make him acceptable in God's sight (*Isa.* 46:12–13).

He is under the power and dominion of sin; sin reigns in and over him; it dwells in every faculty of his soul, and member of his body; so that from head to foot there is no place clean (*Isa.* 1:6; *Rom.* 3:9–18).

He is in the plague-house with Uzziah and excluded from the camp of Israel with the lepers (2 *Chron.* 26:21; *Num.* 5:2; *Job* 36:14).

His 'life is among the unclean'. He is 'in the gall of bitterness, and in the bond of iniquity' (*Acts* 8:28).

He is 'in sin', 'in the flesh', 'in death', 'in the snare of the devil', and is 'taken captive by him at his will' (1 *Cor.* 15:17; *Rom.* 8:8; 1 *John* 3:14; 2 *Tim.* 2:26).

He is under the curse of the law, and the devil dwells in him, and has the mastery of him (*Gal.* 3:13; *Eph.* 2:2,3; *Acts* 26:18).

He is in darkness, and walks in darkness, and knows not where he goes; for darkness has blinded his eyes.

He is in the broad way that leads to destruction; and holding on, he will assuredly go in at the broad gate, and so down the stairs to hell.

2. *What is he that comes not to Jesus Christ?*

He is counted one of God's enemies (*Luke* 19:14; *Rom.* 8:7).

He is a child of the devil, and of hell; for the devil brought him forth, as to his sinful nature, and hell must swallow him at last, because he comes not to Jesus Christ (*John* 8:44; *1 John* 3:8; *Matt.* 23:15; *Psa.* 9:17).

He is a child of wrath, an heir of it; it is his portion, and God will repay it him to his face (*Eph.* 2:1-3; *Job* 21:29–31).

He is a self-murderer; he wrongs his own soul, and is one that loves death (*Prov.* 1:18; 8:36).

He is a companion for devils and damned men (*Prov.* 21:16; *Matt.* 25:41).

3. *Where is he to go that comes not to Jesus Christ?*

He that comes not to him, is like to go further from him; so every sin is a step further from Jesus Christ (*Hos.* 11).

As he is in darkness, so he is like to go on in it; for Christ is the light of the world, and he that comes not to him, walks in darkness (*John* 8:12).

He is like to be removed at last as far from God, and Christ, and heaven, and all felicity, as an infinite God can remove him (*Matt.* 12:41).

Secondly, this doctrine of coming to Christ informs us *where poor destitute sinners may find life for their souls,* and that is in Christ. This life is in his Son; he that has the Son, has life. And again, 'Whoso findeth me findeth life, and shall obtain favour of the LORD' (*Prov.* 8:35). Now, for further enlargement, I will also here offer three more questions: 1. *What life is in Christ?* 2. *Who may have it?* 3. *Upon what terms?*

1. *What life is in Jesus Christ?*

There is justifying life in Christ. Man by sin is dead in law; and Christ only can deliver him by his righteousness and blood from this death into a state of life. 'For God sent his Son into the world, that we might live through him' (*1 John* 4:9). That is, through the righteousness which he should accomplish, and the death that he should die.

There is eternal life in Christ; life that is endless; life for ever and ever. 'He has given us eternal life, and this life is in his Son' (*1 John* 5:11). Now, justification and eternal salvation being both in Christ, and nowhere else to be had for men, who would not come to Jesus Christ?

2. *Who may have this life?*

I answer, poor, helpless, miserable sinners. Particularly:

Such as are willing to have it. 'Whosoever will, let him take the water of life' (*Rev.* 22:17).

He that thirsts for it. 'I will give unto him that is athirst of the fountain of the water of life' (*Rev.* 21:6).

He that is weary of his sins. 'This is the rest wherewith ye may cause the weary to rest; and this is the refreshing' (*Isa.* 28:12).

He that is poor and needy. 'He shall spare the poor and needy, and shall save the souls of the needy' (*Psa.* 72:13).

He that follows after him, and cries for life. 'He that followeth me shall not walk in darkness, but shall have the light of life' (*John* 8:12).

3. *Upon what terms may he have this life?*

Freely. Sinner, do you hear? You may have it freely. Let him take the water of life freely. I will give him of the fountain of the water of life freely. 'And when they had nothing to pay, he frankly forgave them both' (*Luke* 7:42). Freely, without money, or without price. 'Ho! every one that thirsteth, come ye to the waters, and he that hath no money, come ye, buy and eat; yea, come, buy wine and milk without money and without price' (*Isa.* 55:1). Sinner, are you thirsty? Are you weary? Are you willing? Come, then, and regard not your stuff; for all the good that is in Christ is offered to the coming sinner, without money and without price. He has life to give away to such as want it, and that has not a penny to purchase it; and he will give it freely. Oh what a blessed condition is the coming sinner in!

Thirdly, this doctrine of coming to Jesus Christ for life informs us that *it is to be had nowhere else.* If it were to be had anywhere else, the text, and him that spoke it, would be but little respected; for what greater matter is there in, 'I will in no wise cast out', if another stood by that could receive them? But here appears the glory of Christ, that none but he can save. And here appears his love, that though none can save but he, yet he is not slow in saving. 'But him that comes to me', says he, 'I will in no wise cast out.'

That none can save but Jesus Christ, is evident from Acts 4:12: 'Neither is there salvation in any other;' and 'God hath given to us eternal life, and this life is in his Son' (*1 John* 5:11). If life could have been had anywhere else, it should have been in the law. But it is not in the law; for by the deeds of the law, no man living shall be justified; and if not justified, then no life. Therefore life is nowhere to be had but in Jesus Christ (*Gal.* 3).

QUESTION: But why would God so order it, that life should be had nowhere else but in Jesus Christ?

ANSWER: There is reason for it, and that with respect both to God and to us.

1. *With respect to God.*

That it might be in a way of justice as well as mercy. And in a way of justice it could not have been, if it had not been by Christ; because he, and he only, was able to answer the demand of the law, and give for sin what justice required of it.

All angels had been crushed down to hell for ever, had that curse been laid upon them for our sins, which was laid upon Jesus Christ. But it was laid upon him, and he bore it, and answered the penalty, and redeemed his people from under it, with that satisfaction to divine justice that God himself does now proclaim: that he is faithful and just to forgive us, if by faith we shall venture to Jesus, and trust to what he has done for life (*Rom.* 3:24–26; *John* 1:4).

Life must be by Jesus Christ, in order that God might be adored and magnified, for finding out this way. This is the Lord's doing, so that in all things he might be glorified through Jesus Christ our Lord.

It must be by Jesus Christ, that life might be at God's disposal, who has great pity for the poor, the lowly, the meek, the broken in heart, and for those that others do not care for (*Psa.* 34:6; 138:6; 25; 51:17; 147:3).

Life must be in Christ, to cut off boasting from the lips of men. This also is the apostle's reason in Romans 3:19,27 (See also *Eph.* 2:8–10).

2. *Life must be in Jesus Christ with respect to us.*

That we might have it upon the easiest terms, namely, freely as a gift, not as wages. If it was in Moses' hand, we should come hardly at it. If it was in the pope's hand, we should pay soundly for it. But thanks be to God, it is in Christ, laid up in him, and by him to be communicated to sinners upon easy terms, even for receiving, accepting, and embracing with thanksgiving; as the Scriptures plainly declare (*John* 1:11–12; 2 *Cor.* 11:4; *Heb.* 11:13; *Col.* 3:13–15).

Life is in Christ *for us*, that it might not be upon so brittle a foundation as indeed it would had it been anywhere else. The law itself is weak because of us, as to this. But Christ is a tried stone, a sure foundation, one that will not fail to bear your burden, and to receive your soul, coming sinner.

Life is in Christ, that it might be sure to all the seed. Alas! The best of us, if life was left in our hand, to be sure, we should forfeit it, over, and over, and over. Or, if it was in any other hand, we should, by our often backslidings, so offend him, that at last he would shut up his bowels in everlasting displeasure against us. But now it is in Christ, it is with one that can pity, pray for, pardon, yes, multiply pardons. It is with one that can have compassion upon us, when we are out of the way; with one that has a heart to fetch us again, when we are gone astray; with one that can pardon without upbraiding. Blessed be God, that life is in Christ! For now it is sure to all the seed.

Fourthly, this doctrine of coming to Jesus Christ for life informs us of *the evil of unbelief*; that wicked thing that is the only or chief hindrance to the coming sinner. Does the text say, 'Come?' Does it say, 'And him that cometh to me I will in no wise cast out?' Then what an evil that is that keeps sinners from coming to Jesus Christ! And that evil is unbelief: for by faith we come; by unbelief we keep away. Therefore it is said to be that by which a soul departs from God; because it was that which at first caused the world to go away from him, and that also that keeps them from him to this day. And it does it the more easily because it does it with deceit.

Of the Sin of Unbelief

This sin may be called the white devil, for it often, in its mischievous doings in the soul, shows as if it was an angel of light. Yes, it acts like a counsellor of heaven. Therefore a little to discourse of this evil disease.

1. It is that sin, above all others, that has *some show of reason* in its attempts. For it keeps the soul from Christ by pretending its present unfitness and unpreparedness; such as a need of more sense of sin, a need of more repentance, a need of more humility, a need of a more broken heart.

2. It is the sin that *most fits the conscience*. The conscience of the coming sinner tells him that he has nothing good; that he stands indictable for ten thousand talents; that he is a very ignorant, blind, and hard hearted sinner, unworthy to be once taken notice of by Jesus Christ. 'And will you', says Unbelief, 'in such a case as you now are, presume to come to Jesus Christ?'

3. It is the sin that *most fits with our sense of feeling*. The coming sinner feels the workings of sin, of all kinds of sin and wretchedness in his flesh; he also feels the wrath and judgment of God due to sin, and often staggers under it. 'Now,' says Unbelief, 'you may see you have no

grace; for that which works in you is corruption. You may also perceive that God does not love you, because the sense of his wrath abides upon you. Therefore, how can you have the face to come to Jesus Christ?'

4. It is that sin, above all others, that *most fits the wisdom of our flesh*. The wisdom of our flesh thinks it prudent to question awhile, to stand back awhile, to listen to both sides awhile; and not to be rash, sudden, or unadvised in too bold a presuming upon Jesus Christ. And this wisdom unbelief agrees with.

5. It is that sin, above all other, that *continually is whispering in the ear of the soul with mistrust of the faithfulness of God,* in keeping promise to them that come to Jesus Christ for life. It also suggests mistrust about Christ's willingness to receive it, and save it. And no sin can do this so cleverly as unbelief.

6. It is also that sin which is *always at hand to enter an objection* against this or that promise that by the Spirit of God is brought to our heart to comfort us. And if the poor coming sinner is not aware of it, it will, by some evasion, slight, trick, or cavil, quickly wrest from him the promise again, and he shall have but little benefit of it.

7. It is that, above all other sins, that *weakens our prayers, our faith, our love, our diligence, our hope, and expectations*: it even takes the heart away from God in duty.

8. Lastly, this sin *appears in the soul with so many sweet pretences to safety and security*, that it is, as it were, counsel sent from heaven, telling the soul to be wise, wary, considerate, well advised, and to take heed of too rash a venture upon believing. Be sure, first, that God loves you; take hold of no promise until you are forced by God to it; neither be sure of your salvation; doubt it still, though the testimony of the Lord has been often confirmed in you. Live not by faith, but by sense; and when you can neither see nor feel, then fear and mistrust, then doubt and question all.

This is the devilish counsel of unbelief, which is so covered over with specious pretences that the wisest Christian can hardly shake off these reasonings.

ON THE QUALITIES OF UNBELIEF, AS OPPOSED TO FAITH

But to be brief. Let me here give you, Christian reader, a more particular description of the qualities of unbelief, by contrasting it with faith, in these twenty-five particulars:

1. Faith believes the Word of God; but unbelief questions the certainty of the same (*Psa.* 106:24).

2. Faith believes the Word, because it is true; but unbelief doubts it, because it is true (*1 Tim.* 4:3; *John* 8:45).

3. Faith sees more in a promise of God to help than in all other things to hinder; but unbelief, notwithstanding

God's promise, says, How can these things be? (*Rom.* 4:19-21; *2 Kings* 7:2; *John* 3:11-12).

4. Faith will make you see love in the heart of Christ when with his mouth he gives reproofs; but unbelief will imagine wrath in his heart when with his mouth and Word he says he loves us (*Matt.* 15:22-28; *Num.* 13; *Matt.* 25:24).

5. Faith will help the soul to wait, though God defers to give; but unbelief will take the huff and throw up all if God makes any tarrying (*Psa.* 25:5; *Isa.* 8:17; *2 Kings* 6:33; *Psa.* 106:13-14).

6. Faith will give comfort in the midst of fears; but unbelief causes fears in the midst of comfort (*2 Chron.* 20:20-21; *Matt.* 8:26; *Luke* 24:25-27).

7. Faith will suck sweetness out of God's rod; but unbelief can find no comfort in his greatest mercies (*Psa.* 23:4; *Num.* 21).

8. Faith makes great burdens light; but unbelief makes light ones intolerably heavy (*2 Cor.* 4:1, 14-18; *Mal.* 1:12,13).

9. Faith helps us when we are down; but unbelief throws us down when we are up (*Mic.* 7:8-10; *Heb.* 4:11).

10. Faith brings us near to God when we are far from him; but unbelief puts us far from God when we are near to him (*Heb.* 10:22; 3:12–13).

11. Where faith reigns, it declares men to be the friends of God; but where unbelief reigns, it declares them to be his enemies (*James* 2:23; *Heb.* 3:18; *Rev.* 21:8).

12. Faith puts a man under grace; but unbelief holds him under wrath (*Rom.* 3:24-26; *Rom.* 14:6; *Eph.* 2:8; *John* 3:36; *1 John* 5:10; *Heb.* 3:17; *Mark* 16:16).

13. Faith purifies the heart; but unbelief keeps it polluted and impure (*Acts* 15:9; *Titus* 1:15–16).

14. By faith, the righteousness of Christ is imputed to us; but by unbelief, we are shut up under the law to perish (*Rom.* 4:23,24; *Rom.* 11:32; *Gal.* 3:23).

15. Faith makes our work acceptable to God through Christ; but whatsoever is of unbelief is sin. For without faith it is impossible to please him (*Heb.* 11:4; *Rom.* 14:23; *Heb.* 11:6).

16. Faith gives us peace and comfort in our souls; but unbelief works trouble and tossings, like the restless waves of the sea (*Rom.* 5:1; *James* 1:6).

17. Faith makes us see preciousness in Christ; but unbelief sees no form, beauty, or comeliness in him (*1 Pet.* 2:7; *Isa.* 53:1–3).

18. By faith we have our life in Christ's fulness; but by unbelief we starve and pine away (*Gal.* 2:20).

19. Faith gives us the victory over the law, sin, death, the devil, and all evils; but unbelief lays us obnoxious to them all (*1 John* 5:4–5; *Luke* 12:46).

20. Faith will show us more excellence in things not seen than in them that are; but unbelief sees more in things that are seen than in things that will be hereafter (*2 Cor.* 4:18; *Heb.* 11:24–27; *1 Cor.* 15:32).

21. Faith makes the ways of God pleasant and admirable; but unbelief makes them heavy and hard (*Gal.* 5:6; *2 Cor.* 12:10–11; *John* 6:60; *Psa.* 2:3).

22. By faith Abraham, Isaac, and Jacob possessed the land of promise; but because of unbelief, neither Aaron, nor Moses, nor Miriam could get there (*Heb.* 11:9; *Heb.* 3:19).

23. By faith the children of Israel passed through the Red Sea; but by unbelief the generality of them perished in the wilderness (*Heb.* 11:29; *Jude* 5).

24. By faith Gideon did more with three hundred men, and a few empty pitchers than all the twelve tribes could do, because they believed not God (*Judg.* 7:16–22; *Num.* 14:11, 14).

25. By faith Peter walked on the water; but by unbelief he began to sink (*Matt.* 14:28–30).

Thus might many more be added, which, for brevity's sake, I omit; beseeching every one that thinks he has a soul to save, or be damned, to take heed of unbelief, lest, seeing there is a promise left us of entering into his rest, any of us by unbelief should indeed come short of it.

THE SECOND USE: EXAMINATION

We come now to a use of examination. Sinner, you have heard of the necessity of coming to Christ; also of the willingness of Christ to receive the coming soul; together with the benefit that they by him shall have that indeed come to him. Put yourself now upon this serious inquiry, *Am I indeed come to Jesus Christ?*

Motives plenty I might here urge, to prevail with you to a conscientious performance of this duty. As:

You are in sin, in the flesh, in death, in the snare of the devil, and under the curse of the law, if you are not coming to Jesus Christ.

There is no way to be delivered from these, but by coming to Jesus Christ.

If you come, Jesus Christ will receive you, and will in no wise cast you out.

You will not repent it in the day of judgment, if now you come to Jesus Christ.

But you will surely mourn at last, if now you shall refuse to come.

And lastly, now you have been invited to come; now will your judgment be greater, and your damnation more fearful, if you shall yet refuse, than if you had never heard of coming to Christ.

OBJECTION: But we hope we have come to Jesus Christ.

ANSWER: It is well if it proves so. But lest you should speak without ground, and so fall unawares into hell fire, let us examine a little.

1. *Firstly, are you indeed come to Jesus Christ? What have you left behind you? What did you come away from, in your coming to Jesus Christ?*

When Lot came out of Sodom, he left the Sodomites behind him (*Gen.* 19). When Abraham came out of Chaldea, he left his country and kindred behind him (*Gen.* 12; *Acts* 7). When Ruth came to put her trust under the wings of the LORD God of Israel, she left her father and mother, her gods, and the land of her nativity, behind her (*Ruth* 1:15–17; 2:11–12). When Peter came to Christ, he left his nets behind him (*Matt.* 4:20). When Zacchæus came to Christ, he left the receipt of custom behind him (*Luke* 19). When Paul came to Christ, he left his own righteousness behind him (*Phil.* 3:7–8). When those that used curious arts came to Jesus Christ, they took their curious books and burned them; though, in another man's eye, they were counted worth fifty thousand pieces of silver (*Acts* 19:18–20).

What do you say, man? Have you left your darling sins, your Sodomitish pleasures, your acquaintance and vain companions, your unlawful gain, your idol gods, your righteousness, and your unlawful curious arts, behind you? If any of these are with you, and you with them, in your heart and life, you are not yet come to Jesus Christ.

2. *Secondly, are you come to Jesus Christ? Pray tell me what moved you to come to Jesus Christ?*

Men do not usually come or go to this or that place, before they have a moving cause, or rather a cause moving them there. No more do they come to Jesus Christ – I do not say, before they have a cause, but – before that cause moves them to come. What do you say? Have you a cause moving you to come? To be at present in a state of condemnation is cause sufficient for men to come to Jesus Christ for life. But that will not do, except the cause move them; which it will never do, until their eyes be opened to see themselves in that condition. For it is not a man's being under wrath, but his seeing it, that moves him to come to Jesus Christ. Alas! All men by sin are under wrath; yet but few of that all come to Jesus Christ. And the reason is, because they do not see their condition. 'Who hath warned you to flee from the wrath to come?' (*Matt.* 3:7). Until men are warned, and also receive the warning, they will not come to Jesus Christ.

Take three or four examples of this. Adam and Eve did not come to Jesus Christ until they received the alarm, the conviction of their undone state by sin (*Gen.* 3) The children of Israel did not cry out for a mediator before they saw themselves in danger of death by the law (*Exod.* 20:18–19). Before the publican came, he saw himself lost and undone (*Luke* 18:13). The prodigal did not come, until he saw death at the door, ready to devour him (*Luke* 15:17–18). The three thousand came not, until they knew not what to do to be saved (*Acts* 2:37–39). Paul came not, until he saw himself lost and undone (*Acts* 9:3–8,11). Lastly, before the jailer came, he saw himself undone (*Acts* 16:29–31).

And I tell you, it is an easier thing to persuade a healthy man to go to the physician for cure, or a man without hurt to seek for a plaster to cure him, than it is to persuade a man that sees not his soul diseased, to come to Jesus Christ. The whole have no need of the physician. Then why should they go to him? The full pitcher can hold no more. Then why should it go to the fountain? And if you come full, you come not aright; and be sure Christ will send you empty away. 'But he healeth the broken in heart, and bindeth up their wounds' (*Mark* 2:17; *Psa.* 147:3; *Luke* 1:53).

3. *Thirdly, are you coming to Jesus Christ? Pray tell me, what do you see in him to allure you to forsake all the world, to come to him?*

I say, What have you seen in him? Men must see something in Jesus Christ, or they will not come to him.

What comeliness have you seen in his person? You will not come if you see no form nor comeliness in him (*Isa.* 53:1–3).

Until those mentioned in the Song of Solomon were convinced that there was more beauty, comeliness, and desirableness in Christ than in ten thousand, they did not so much as ask where he was, nor incline to turn aside after him (*Song of Sol.* 5, 6).

There be many things on this side of heaven that can and do carry away the heart; and so will do, so long as you live, if you shall be kept blind, and not be admitted to see the beauty of the Lord Jesus.

4. *Fourthly, are you come to the Lord Jesus? What have you found in him, since you came to him?*

Peter found in him the words of eternal life (*John* 6:68). They that Peter mentions found him a living stone, even such a living stone as communicated life to them (*1 Pet.* 2:4–5). He says himself, they that come to him shall find rest unto their souls. Have you found rest in him for your soul (*Matt.* 11:28)?

Let us go back to the times of the Old Testament.

1. *Abraham* found that in him that made him leave his country for him, and become for his sake a pilgrim and stranger in the earth (*Gen.* 12; *Heb.* 11).

2. *Moses* found that in him that made him forsake a crown, and a kingdom for him too.

3. *David* found so much in him that he counted to be in his house one day was better than a thousand; yes, to be a door-keeper there was better, in his esteem, than to dwell in the tents of wickedness (*Psa.* 84:10).

4. What did *Daniel and the three children* find in him, to make them run the hazards of the fiery furnace, and the den of lions, for his sake? (*Dan.* 3–6).

Let us come down to martyrs.

1. *Stephen* found that in him that made him joyful, and quietly yielded up his life for his Name (*Acts* 7).

2. *Ignatius* found that in Christ that made him choose to go through the torments of the devil, and hell itself, rather than not to have him.[1]

3. What saw *Romanus* in Christ, when he said to the raging Emperor who threatened him with fearful torments, 'Your sentence, O Emperor, I joyfully embrace, and refuse not to be sacrificed by as cruel torments as you can invent'?[2]

4. What saw *Menas*, the Egyptian, in Christ, when he said, under most cruel torments, 'There is nothing in my mind that can be compared to the kingdom of heaven; neither is all the world, if it was weighed in a balance, to be preferred above the price of one soul? Who is able to separate us from the love of Jesus Christ our Lord? And I have learned of my Lord and King not to fear them that kill the body', etc.[3]

5. What did *Eulalia* see in Christ, when she said, as they were pulling her one joint from another, 'Behold, O Lord, I will not forget thee. What a pleasure it is for them, O Christ, that remember thy triumphant victory!'?[4]

---

[1] Foxe's *Acts & Monuments* (1632 edition), vol. 1, p. 52.
[2] Ibid., p. 116.   [3] Ibid., p. 117.   [4] Ibid., p. 121.

6. What do you think *Agnes* saw in Christ, when rejoicingly she went to meet the soldier that was appointed to be her executioner. 'I will willingly', said she, 'receive into my paps the length of this sword, and into my breast will draw the force of it, even to the hilts; that thus I, being married to Christ my spouse, may surmount and escape all the darkness of this world'?[5]

7. What, do you think, did *Julitta* see in Christ, when, at the Emperor's telling of her, that except she would worship the gods, she should never have protection, laws, judgments, nor life, she replied, 'Farewell life, welcome death; farewell riches, welcome poverty: all that I have, if it were a thousand times more, would I rather lose, than to speak one wicked and blasphemous word against my Creator'?[6]

8. What did *Marcus Arethusius* see in Christ, when after his enemies had cut his flesh, anointed it with honey, and hanged him up in a basket for flies and bees to feed on, he would not give, to uphold idolatry, one halfpenny to save his life?[7]

9. What did *Constantine* see in Christ, when he used to kiss the wounds of those that suffered for him?[8]

10. But why give these particular examples of words and smaller actions, when by their lives, their blood, their enduring hunger, sword, fire, pulling asunder, and all

[5] Ibid., p. 122. [6] Ibid., p. 123. [7] Ibid., p. 128. [8] Ibid., p. 135.

torments that the devil and hell could devise, for the love they bore to Christ, after they were come to him?

What have YOU found in him, sinner? What! Come to Christ, and find nothing in him? – when all things that are worth looking after are in him! – or if anything, yet not enough to wean you from your sinful delights, and fleshly lusts! Away, away, *you* have not come to Jesus Christ. He that has come to Jesus Christ has found in him that, as I said, that is not to be found anywhere else.

1. He that is come to Christ has found God in him reconciling the world to himself, not imputing their trespasses to them. And so God is not to be found in heaven and earth besides (*2 Cor.* 5:19–20).

2. He that is come to Jesus Christ has found in him a fountain of grace, sufficient, not only to pardon sin, but to sanctify the soul, and to preserve it from falling, in this evil world.

3. He that is come to Jesus Christ has found virtue in him; *that* virtue, that if he but touches you with his Word, or you him by faith, life is immediately conveyed into your soul. It makes you wake as one that is woken out of his sleep; it awakes all the powers of the soul (*Psa.* 30:11–12; *Song of Sol.* 6:12).

4. Have you come to Jesus Christ? You have found glory in him, glory that surmounts and goes beyond. 'Thou art more glorious and excellent than the mountains of prey' (*Psa.* 76:4).

5. What shall I say? You have found righteousness in him; you have found rest, peace, delight, heaven, glory, and eternal life.

Sinner, be advised; ask your heart again, saying, 'Am I come to Jesus Christ?' For upon this one question, 'Am I come, or, am I not?', hangs your heaven and hell. If you can say, 'I have come', and God shall approve that saying, happy, happy, happy man are you! But if you have not come, what can make you happy? Yes, what can make that man happy that, for his not coming to Jesus Christ for life, must be damned in hell?

THE THIRD USE: ENCOURAGEMENT

Coming sinner, I have now a word for you. Be of good comfort, 'He will in no wise cast out.' Of all men, you are the blessed of the Lord; the Father has prepared his Son to be a sacrifice for you, and Jesus Christ, your Lord, is gone to prepare a place for you (*John* 1:29; *John* 14:2–3; *Heb.* 10). What shall I say to you?

Firstly, you come to a FULL Christ.
You cannot want anything for soul or body, for this world or that to come, but it is to be had in or by Jesus Christ. As it was said of the land that the Danites went to possess (*Judg.* 18:10), so, and with much more truth, it may be said of Christ: he is such a one that with him there is no want of any good thing that is in heaven or earth. A full Christ is your Christ.

1. *He is full of grace.* Grace is sometimes taken for love: never any loved like Jesus Christ. Jonathan's love went beyond the love of women; but the love of Christ passes knowledge. It is beyond the love of all the earth, of all creatures, even of men and angels. His love prevailed with him to lay aside his glory, to leave the heavenly place, to clothe himself with flesh, to be born in a stable, to be laid in a manger, to live a poor life in the world, to take upon him our sicknesses, infirmities, sins, curse, death, and the wrath that was due to man.

And all this he did for a base, undeserving, unthankful people; yes, for a people that was at enmity with him. 'For when we were yet without strength, in due time Christ died for the ungodly. For scarcely for a righteous man will one die; yet peradventure for a good man some would even dare to die. But God commendeth his love toward us, in that while we were yet sinners, Christ died for us. Much more, then, being now justified by his blood, we shall be saved from wrath through him. For if, when we were enemies, we were reconciled to God by the death of his Son, much more, being reconciled, we shall be saved by his life' (*Rom.* 5:6–10).

2. *He is full of truth.* 'Full of grace and truth.' Truth, that is, faithfulness in keeping promise, even this of the text, with all others, 'I will in no wise cast out' (*John* 14:6). Hence it is said, that his words are true, and that he is the faithful God that keeps covenant. And hence it is also that his promises are called truth: 'Thou wilt perform

the truth to Jacob, and the mercy to Abraham, which thou hast sworn unto our fathers from the days of old' (*Mic.* 7:20). Therefore it is said again that both himself and his words are truth: 'I am the truth', 'the Scripture of truth' (*Dan.* 10:21). 'Thy word is truth,' (*John* 17:17; 2 *Sam.* 7:28). 'Thy law is the truth' (*Psa.* 119:142); and 'My mouth', says he, 'shall speak truth' (*Prov.* 8:7); see also *Eccles.* 12:10; *Isa.* 25:1; *Mal.* 2:6; *Acts* 26:25; 2 *Tim.* 2:12–13.

Now, I say, his word is truth, and he is full of truth to fulfil his truth, even to a thousand generations. Coming sinner, he will not deceive you. Come boldly to Jesus Christ.

3. *He is full of wisdom.* He is made unto us of God wisdom; wisdom to manage the affairs of his church in general, and the affairs of every coming sinner in particular. And upon this account he is said to be 'head over all things' (*1 Cor.* 1:30; *Eph* 1:22), because he manages all things that are in the world by his wisdom, for the good of his church.

All men's actions, all Satan's temptations, all God's providences, all crosses, and disappointments; all things whatever are under the hand of Christ – who is the wisdom of God – and he orders them all for good to his church. And if Christ can help it – and you may be sure he can – nothing shall happen or fall out in the world but it shall, despite all opposition, have a good tendency to his church and people.

4. *He is full of the Spirit*, to communicate him to the coming sinner; he has therefore received him without measure, that he may communicate him to every member of his body, according as every man's measure thereof is allotted him by the Father. Therefore he says, that he that comes to him, 'Out of his belly shall flow rivers of living water' (*John* 3:34; *Titus* 3:5–6; *Acts* 2:33; *John* 7:33–39).

5. *He is indeed a storehouse full of all the graces of the Spirit.* 'Of his fulness have all we received, and grace for grace' (*John* 1:16). Here is more faith, more love, more sincerity, more humility, more of every grace; and of this, even more of this, he gives to every lowly, humble, penitent coming sinner. Therefore, coming soul, you do not come to a barren wilderness when you come to Jesus Christ.

6. *He is full of bowels and compassion:* and they shall feel and find it so that come to him for life. He can bear with your weaknesses, he can pity your ignorance, he can be touched with the feeling of your infirmities, he can affectionately forgive your transgressions, he can heal your backslidings, and love you freely.

His compassions fail not; 'and he will not break a bruised reed, nor quench the smoking flax; he can pity them that no eye pities, and be afflicted in all your afflictions' (*Matt.* 26:41; *Heb.* 5:2; 2:18; *Matt.* 9:2; *Hos.* 14:4; *Ezek.* 16:5–6; *Isa.* 63:9; *Psa.* 78:38; 86:15; 111:4; 112:4; *Lam.* 3:22; *Isa.* 42:3).

7. Coming soul, *the Jesus that you are coming to, is full of might and terribleness for your advantage.* He can suppress all your enemies; he is the Prince of the kings of the earth; he can bow all men's designs for your help; he can break all snares laid for you in the way; he can lift you out of all the difficulties with which you may be surrounded.

He is wise in heart, and mighty in power. Every life under heaven is in his hand; yes, the fallen angels tremble before him. And he will save your life, coming sinner (*1 Cor.* 1:24; *Rom.* 8:28; *Matt.* 28:18; *Rev.* 4; *Psa.* 19:3; 27:5,6; *Job* 9:4; *John* 17:2; *Matt.* 8:29; *Luke* 8:28; *James* 2:19).

8. Coming sinner, *the Jesus to whom you are coming is lowly in heart, he does not despise any.* It is not your outward meanness, nor your inward weakness; it is not because you are poor, or base, or deformed, or a fool, that he will despise you: he has chosen the foolish, the base, and despised things of this world, to confound the wise and mighty.

He will bow his ear to your stammering prayers. He will pick out the meaning of your inexpressible groans; he will respect your weakest offering, if there be in it but your heart (*Matt.* 11:20; *Luke* 14:21; *Prov.* 9:4-6; *Isa.* 38: 14–15; *Song of Sol.* 5:15; *John* 4:27; *Mark* 12:33–34; *James* 5:11). Now, is this not a blessed Christ, coming sinner? Will you not do well, when you have embraced him, coming sinner?

Secondly, you have yet another advantage by Jesus Christ, you who are coming to him, for *he is not only full but free.* He is not sparing of what he has; he is open hearted and open handed. Let me in a few particulars show you this:

1. This is evident, because *he calls you; he calls upon you to come to him; which he would not do, was he not free to give;* yes, he bids you, when you come, to ask, seek, knock. And for your encouragement, adds to every command a promise, 'Ask, and it shall be given you; seek, and ye shall find; knock, and it shall be opened unto you.' If the rich man should say thus to the poor, would not he be reckoned a free-hearted man? I say, should he say to the poor, 'Come to my door, ask at my door, knock at my door, and you shall find and have'; would he not be counted liberal? Why, thus does Jesus Christ. Mind it, coming sinner (*Isa.* 55:3; *Psa.* 50:15; *Matt.* 7:7–9).

2. *He does not only bid you come, but tells you, he will heartily do you good;* yes, he will do it with rejoicing; 'I will rejoice over them, to do them good . . . with my whole heart, and with my whole soul' (*Jer.* 32:41).

3. It appeareth that he is free, because *he gives without reproaching.* 'He giveth to all men liberally, and upbraideth not' (*James* 1:5). There are some that will not deny to do the poor a pleasure, but they will mix their mercies with so many rebukes, that the persons on whom

they bestow their charity shall find very little sweetness in it. But Christ does not do so, coming sinner; he casts all your iniquities behind his back (*Isa.* 38:17). Your sins and iniquities he will remember no more (*Heb.* 8:12).

4. *That Christ is free, is manifest by the complaints that he makes against them that will not come to him for mercy.* I say, he complains, saying, 'O Jerusalem, Jerusalem! How often would I have gathered your children together, even as a hen gathereth her chickens under her wings, and ye would not!' (*Matt.* 23:37). I say, he speaks it by way of complaint. He says also in another place, 'But thou hast not called upon me, O Jacob' (*Isa.* 43:22). Coming sinner, see here the willingness of Christ to save; see here how free he is to communicate life, and all good things, to such as you.

He complains, if you come not; he is displeased, if you call not upon him. Hark, coming sinner, once again; when Jerusalem would not come to him for safeguard, 'He beheld the city, and wept over it, saying, If thou hadst known, even thou, at least in this thy day, the things which belong unto thy peace; but now they are hid from thine eyes' (*Luke* 19:41–42).

5. Lastly, *He is open and free hearted to do you good, as is seen by the joy and rejoicing that he manifests at the coming home of poor prodigals.* He receives the lost sheep with rejoicing; the lost coin with rejoicing; yes, when the prodigal came home, what joy and mirth, what music and dancing, was in his father's house (*Luke* 15)!

Thirdly, coming sinner, I will add another encouragement for your help.

1. *God has prepared a mercy-seat, a throne of grace to sit on;* that you may come there to him, and that he may from there hear you, and receive you. 'I will commune with you,' says he, 'from above the mercy-seat' (*Exod.* 25:22). As if he said, Sinner, when you come to me, you shall find me upon the mercy-seat, where also I am always found of the undone coming sinner. There I bring my pardons; there I hear and receive their petitions, and accept them to my favour.

2. *God has also prepared a golden altar for you to offer your prayers and tears upon.* A golden altar! It is called a *golden* altar, to show what worth it is in God's account: for this golden altar is Jesus Christ; this altar sanctifies your gift, and makes your sacrifice acceptable. This altar, then, makes your groans *golden groans*; your tears *golden tears*; and your prayers *golden prayers*, in the eye of that God you come to, coming sinner (*Rev.* 8; *Matt.* 23:19; *Heb.* 10:10; *1 Pet.* 2:5).

3. *God has strewed all the way, from the gate of hell, where you were, to the gate of heaven, where you are going, with flowers out of his own garden.* Behold how the promises, invitations, calls, and encouragements, like lilies, lie round about you! Take heed that you do not tread them under foot, sinner. With promises, did I say?

Yes, he has mixed all those with his own Name, his Son's Name; also, with the name of mercy, goodness, compassion, love, pity, grace, forgiveness, pardon, and what not, that may encourage the coming sinner.

4. *He has also for your encouragement laid up the names, and set forth the sins, of those that have been saved.* In his book they are fairly written, that you, through patience and comfort of the Scriptures, might have hope.

In this book is recorded *Noah's* name and sin; and how God had mercy upon him.

In this record is fairly written the name of *Lot*, and the nature of his sin; and how the Lord had mercy upon him.

In this record you have also fairly written the names of *Moses, Aaron, Gideon, Samson, David, Solomon, Peter, Paul,* with the nature of their sins; and how God had mercy upon them; and all to encourage you, coming sinner.

Fourthly, I will add yet another encouragement for the man that is coming to Jesus Christ. Are you coming? Are you coming, indeed?

1. Then this your coming is *by virtue of God's call.* You are called. Calling goes before coming. Coming is not of works, but of him that calls. 'He goeth up into a mountain, and calleth unto him whom he would; and they came unto him' (*Mark* 3:13).

2. Are you coming? *This is also by virtue of illumin-ation.* God has made you see; and, therefore, you are coming. So long as you were darkness, you loved dark-ness and could not abide to come, because your deeds were evil; but being now illuminated and made to see what and where you are, and also what and where your Saviour is, now you are coming to Jesus Christ. 'Blessed art thou, Simon Bar-jona: for flesh and blood has not revealed it unto thee,' says Christ, 'but my Father which is in heaven' (*Matt.* 16:17).

3. Are you coming? *This is because God has inclined your heart to come.* God has called you, illuminated you, and inclined your heart to come; and, therefore, you come to Jesus Christ. It is God that works in you to will, and to come to Jesus Christ. Coming sinner, bless God that he has given you a will to come to Jesus Christ. It is a sign that you belong to Jesus Christ, because God has made you willing to come to him (*Psa.* 110:3). Bless God for slaying the enmity of your mind; had he not done it, you would still be hating your own salvation.

4. Are you coming to Jesus Christ? *It is God that gives you power:* power to pursue your will in the matters of your salvation is the gift of God. 'It is God which worketh in you both to will and to do' (*Phil.* 2:13). Not that God works a will to come where he gives no power; but you should take notice, that power is an additional mercy. The church saw that will and power were two things when she

cried, 'Draw me, we will run after thee' (*Song of Sol.* 1:4). And so did David too, when he said, 'I will run the way of thy commandments, when thou shalt enlarge my heart' (*Psa.* 119:32). Will to come, and power to pursue your will, is double mercy, coming sinner.

5. *All your strange, passionate, sudden rushings forward after Jesus Christ* (coming sinners know what I mean), *they also are your helps from God.* Perhaps you feel, at some times more than at others, strong stirrings up of heart to fly to Jesus Christ. You have at those times a sweet and stiff gale of the Spirit of God filling your sails with the fresh winds of his good Spirit; and you ride at those times as upon the wings of the wind, being carried out beyond yourself, beyond the most of your prayers, and also above all your fear and temptations.

6. Coming sinner, *have you not now and then a kiss of the sweet lips of Jesus Christ,* I mean some blessed word dropping like a honey-comb upon your soul to revive you, when you are in the midst of your dumps?

7. *Does not Jesus Christ sometimes give you a glimpse of himself,* though perhaps you see him not for so long a time as while one may count to twenty.

8. *Have you not sometimes as it were the very warmth of his wings overshadowing the face of your soul,* giving a glow upon your spirit, as the bright beams of the sun do

upon your body, when it suddenly breaks out of a cloud, though presently all is gone away?

Well, all these things are the good hand of your God upon you, and they are upon you to constrain, to provoke, and to make you willing and able to come, coming sinner, that you might in the end be saved.

Analysis

Chapter 1: THE CONTEXT AND THE TEXT

The context – John 6
The text – John 6:37
    i. The gift of the Father to the Son
   ii. The Son's reception of the Father's gift

Chapters 2–5: EXPLANATION OF THE TEXT

CHAPTER 2: The extent of the gift: *All*
               The person giving: *the Father*
               The meaning of the word *giveth*
               The Father's purpose in giving
CHAPTER 3: The Son's reception of the gift: *shall come*
               What it is to come to Christ
               Objections in the way of coming to Christ
                    Six objections considered
               The force of the promise to those coming
                    In general
                    In particular

Chapters 2–5: EXPLANATION OF THE TEXT

CHAPTER 3 (continued):
>   Objections to the absoluteness of the promise
>>   Seven objections considered

CHAPTER 4
>   What the words *to me* imply
>>   The all-sufficiency of Christ
>>   Those who come receive from Christ
>   The promise to those coming to Christ
>   How the one that has come to Christ benefits
>   The meaning of the word *cometh*

CHAPTER 5
>   Two sorts of sinners come to Christ
>>   The newly-awakened comer
>>   The returning backslider
>>>   Objections of backsliders answered
>   The importance of the words *to me*
>   The meaning of the words *in no wise*
>   The meaning of the words *cast out*
>>   What it is to cast out
>>   The power of Christ to save or cast out

Chapters 6 & 7: OBSERVATIONS ON THE TEXT

CHAPTER 6:

Observation 1: *Coming to Christ is by the gift, promise and drawing of the Father*

Use and Application of Observation 1
Five Uses and two Objections considered

CHAPTER 7:

Observation 2: *Those coming are often afraid that Christ will not receive them*

Seven Causes of these fears considered
Temptations in this connection, and the reasons for them

Application of Observation 2
Four implications considered

Observation 3: *Christ would not have those who come think that he will not receive them*
Three proofs of this
Nine reasons for Observation 3

Chapter 8: APPLICATION OF THE DOCTRINE

FIRST USE: Information
>   Men by nature are far from Christ
>   Sinners may find life for their souls in Christ
>   Life is to be had nowhere else
>   Of the sin of unbelief
> >   Twenty-five properties of unbelief,
> >   as opposed to faith

SECOND USE: Examination
>   Am I indeed come to Jesus Christ?
> >   What have I left behind?
> >   What moved me to come?
> >   What do I see in him to allure me?
> >   What have I found in him?

THIRD USE: Encouragement
>   Sinners come to a full Christ
>   Sinners come to a free Christ
>   Four further encouragements from Scripture
>   Eight final encouragements to those coming
>   to Christ